Taking Off

Beginning English

Susan Hancock Fesler
Christy M. Newman

Taking Off Beginning English, First Edition

Published by McGraw-Hill/Contemporary, a business unit of The McGraw-Hill Companies,
Inc., 1221 Avenue of the Americas, New York, NY 10020. Copyright © 2003 by The McGraw-Hill
Companies, Inc. All rights reserved. No part of this publication may be reproduced or distributed
in any form or by any means, or stored in a database or retrieval system, without the prior written
consent of The McGraw-Hill Companies, Inc., including, but not limited to, in any network or
other electronic storage or transmission, or broadcast for distance learning.

7 8 9 0 QPD 0 9 8 7 6 (Student Book)
ISBN 13: 978-0-07-282063-8
ISBN 10: 0-07-282063-2

1 2 3 4 5 6 7 8 9 QPD 11 10 09 08 07 06
ISBN 13: 978-0-07-326256-7 (Student Book with Audio Highlights)
ISBN 10: 0-07-326256-0

Editorial director: Tina B. Carver
Senior managing editor: Erik Gundersen
Developmental editors: Karen P. Hazar, Linda O'Roke
Director of North American marketing: Thomas P. Dare
Director of international sales and marketing: Kate Oakes
Production manager: Juanita Thompson
Cover designer: Michael Kelly
Interior designer: Eileen Wagner
Art: Anna DiVito, Phil Scheuer, and Leap'n Lizards Design
Skills indexer: Talbot Hamlin

 McGraw-Hill

www.esl-elt.mcgraw-hill.com

The McGraw-Hill Companies

Acknowledgements

The authors and publisher would like to thank the following individuals who reviewed the *Taking Off* program at various stages of development and whose comments, reviews, and assistance were instrumental in helping us shape the project:

Sally Gearhart
Santa Rosa Junior College
Santa Rosa, CA

Maria Elena Gonzalez
Adult Literacy Resource Institute
University of Massachusetts, Boston
Boston, MA

LaRanda Marr
Office of Adult Education
Oakland Unified School District
Oakland, CA

Anne Molina
Evans Community Adult School
Los Angeles Unified School District
Los Angeles, CA

Patricia Mooney-Gonzalez
New York State Department of Education
Albany, NY

Paula Orias
Piper Community School
Broward County Public Schools
Sunrise, FL

Rachel Porcelli
Memphis City Schools
Memphis, TN

Sylvia Ramirez
Community Learning Center
MiraCosta College
Oceanside, CA

Kristin Sherman
Adult ESL Program
Central Piedmont Community College
Charlotte, NC

Mary Ann Siegel
Albany Park Community Center
Chicago, IL

Lynda Terrill
Center for Applied Linguistics
Washington, DC

Dave VanLew
Simi Valley Adult & Career Institute
Simi Valley, CA

I would like to thank all of those friends and colleagues who helped and encouraged me with this text. Thanks to Christy Newman for being a consummate professional and tireless co-author. A special thanks to Tina Carver for her friendship and guidance over the years. Deep appreciation to Tracy D. Terrell and Jeanne Egasse for their vision and inspiration regarding the language acquisition process. And, of course, my gratitude to my family for their love, encouragement, and understanding.

— Susan Hancock Fesler

I would like to thank Susan Fesler for inviting me to join her on this project and for her friendship. I want to thank Karen Hazar, Linda O'Roke, and Mari Vargo, editors *par excellence*. I also owe a great deal to Erik Gundersen for his vision, insight, and understanding of what works. And finally, thanks to Tom, Corey, and Jonathan for everything else.

— Christy M. Newman

To the Teacher

Taking Off is a four-skills, standards-based program for low beginning students of English. Picture dictionary art pages teach life-skills vocabulary in a clear and visual way. The gradual pace of the course instills confidence in students as they establish a solid foundation in the basics of English.

Features

- **Four-skills foundation course** prepares students for Book 1 in a variety of popular series.

- **Activities correlated to CASAS, SCANS, EFF, and other key standards** prepare students to master a broad range of critical competencies.

- **Picture dictionary art pages** highlight life-skills vocabulary in engaging contexts.

- **Listening preparation activities** help students develop speaking, reading, and writing skills in a low-anxiety environment.

- **A *Numbers* page in each unit** helps students build numeracy skills for basic math work.

- ***In the Community* lessons** introduce students to critical civics topics.

- ***Grammar Spotlights*** present a small set of basic grammar points.

- **Literacy Workbook** provides reading and writing "on-ramp" activities for emerging readers and writers.

Components

- **Student Book** has twelve 12-page units with a wealth of individual, pair-, and group-work activities. In four special sections throughout the book, students and teachers will also find *Grammar Spotlight* and *Review* lessons for additional study and practice. Listening scripts are found at the back of the Student Book and in the Teacher's Edition.

- **Teacher's Edition with Tests** provides the following resources for each unit in the Student Book:
    - Step-by-step teaching instructions
    - Five to seven expansion activities
    - Two-page test
    - Listening scripts for all audio program materials
    - Answer keys for Student Book, Workbook, Literacy Workbook, and test materials.

- **Color Transparencies** provide full-color acetates for unit-opening scenes in the Student Book.

- **Audiocassettes and Audio CDs for Student Book** contain recordings for all listening activities in the Student Book. Listening passages for each unit test are provided at the end of the audio section for that unit.

- **Workbook** includes supplementary practice for students who have basic reading and writing skills in their first language.

- **Literacy Workbook** provides reading and writing "on ramp" activities for emerging readers and writers. This component is designed for students who do *not* have foundational literacy skills in their first language. Like the Workbook, the Literacy Workbook offers supplementary activities for each unit in the Student Book.

- **Literacy Workbook Audiocassette and Audio CD** provide additional listening practice.

PROGRAM OVERVIEW

Guide to *Taking Off*

Consult the *Guide to Taking Off* on pages xvi-xix. This Guide offers teachers and program directors a visual tour of one Student Book unit.

Predictable lesson format

Most of the lessons in the Student Book are one page in length and contain three to five activities. This one-page lesson format allows teachers to "chunk" their instruction into short, manageable sections, allowing students to quickly complete lessons and feel a sense of accomplishment. The first activity in most lessons asks students to listen to and repeat new vocabulary and language. These listen and repeat activities help students prepare for speaking, reading, and writing skills in a low-anxiety environment. At the low beginning level, it is critical that students have a chance to listen to and repeat all new vocabulary and language before being asked to speak, read, or write.

Recurring cast of multicultural characters

Taking Off features an engaging cast of characters enrolled in a beginning English class. The authors developed the book around these characters to help students learn new language from familiar and engaging faces. Here is a profile of the characters in *Taking Off*:

Character	Nationality
Sandy Johnson (teacher)	American
Carlos Avila	Brazilian
Maria Cruz	Mexican
Leo Danov	Russian
Don Park	Korean
Tien Lam	Vietnamese
Grace Lee	Chinese
Paul Lemat	Haitian
Isabel Lopez	Colombian

Unit-opening illustrations

Each unit opens with a dynamic, full-page illustration, providing context for the key vocabulary items and language presented in the unit. This illustration sets the scene for the unit, activating students' background knowledge and encouraging them to share words they can say in English. Teachers can present the unit-opening illustrations on an overhead projector with the Color Transparencies.

CASAS, SCANS, EFF, and other standards

Program directors and teachers are often asked to benchmark student progress against national and/or state standards. With this in mind, *Taking Off* carefully integrates instructional elements from a wide range of standards including CASAS, SCANS, and EFF. Here is a brief overview of our approach to meeting these standards:

- **CASAS.** Many U.S. states tie funding for adult education programs to student performance on the Comprehensive Adult Student Assessment System (CASAS). The CASAS (www.casas.org) competencies identify more than 300 essential skills that adults need in order to succeed in the classroom, workplace, and community. Examples of these skills include: identifying or using appropriate non-verbal behavior in a variety of settings, responding appropriately to common personal information questions, and comparing price or quality to determine the best buys. *Taking Off* carefully integrates CASAS competencies that are appropriate for low beginning students.

- **SCANS.** Developed by the U.S. Department of Labor, SCANS is an acronym for the Secretary's Commission on Achieving Necessary Skills (www.wdr.doleta.gov/SCANS/). SCANS competencies are workplace skills that help people compete more effectively in today's global economy. The following are examples of SCANS competencies: works well with others, acquires and evaluates information, and teaches others new skills. A variety of SCANS competencies are threaded throughout the activities in each unit of *Taking Off*. The incorporation of these competencies recognizes both the intrinsic importance of teaching workplace skills and the fact that many adult students at the low beginning level are already working members of their communities.

- **EFF.** Equipped for the Future (EFF) is a set of standards for adult literacy and lifelong learning, developed by the National Institute for Literacy (www.nifl.gov). The organizing principle of EFF is that adults assume responsibilities in three major areas of life — as parents, citizens, and workers. These three areas of focus are called "role maps" in the EFF documentation. In the parent role map, for example, EFF addresses these and other responsibilities: participating in children's formal education and forming and maintaining supportive family relationships. Each *Taking Off* unit addresses one or more of the EFF role maps. The focus on the student as community citizen is particularly strong in Lesson 9 of each unit, which is devoted to *In the Community* activities.

Number of hours of instruction

The *Taking Off* program has been designed to accommodate the needs of adult classes with 96-216 hours of classroom instruction. Here are three recommended ways in which various components in the *Taking Off* program can be combined to meet student and teacher needs:

- **96-120 hours.** Teachers are encouraged to work through all of the Student Book materials, incorporating the *Grammar Spotlights* and *Review* lessons as time permits. The Color Transparencies can be used to introduce and/or review materials in each unit. Teachers should also look to the Teacher's Edition for teaching suggestions and testing materials as necessary.

  Time per unit: 8-10 hours.

- **120-168 hours.** In addition to working through all of the Student Book materials, teachers are encouraged to incorporate the Workbook and/or Literacy Workbook for supplementary practice.

  Time per unit: 10-14 hours.

- **168-216 hours.** Teachers and students working in an intensive instructional setting can take advantage of the wealth of expansion activities threaded through the Teacher's Edition to supplement their use of the Student Book and Workbook materials.

  Time per unit: 14-18 hours.

Assessment

Some teachers prefer to evaluate their students informally by monitoring their students' listening and speaking abilities during pair-work or group-work activities. These teachers may also maintain portfolios of student writing to show the progress students are making in writing skill development.

For teachers who need or want formal assessments of their students, the Teacher's Edition provides two-page, reproducible tests for each Student Book unit. Each test takes approximately 30 minutes to administer, and these tests are designed to assess vocabulary acquisition and listening comprehension skills. There are two listening activities on each test, and the recorded passages for these sections are found on the Student Book Audiocassettes and Audio CDs. Listening scripts for the tests appear in the Teacher's Edition.

SPECIAL FEATURES

Grammar Spotlights

Fundamental grammar points like the simple present tense of BE and HAVE are presented throughout the Student Book in two-page *Grammar Spotlight* lessons. These lessons appear at regular intervals throughout the book, but are not incorporated into the units themselves. In this way, teachers who address grammar in a direct way can call their students' attention to the *Grammar Spotlights* and to the corresponding grammar practice in the Workbook. Teachers who prefer not to present and practice grammar with their low beginning students can skip the *Grammar Spotlights*.

Numeracy skills for basic math

Learning basic math skills is critically important for success in school, on the job, and at home. As such, most national and state-level standards for adult education mandate instruction in basic math skills. With this in mind, Lesson 8 in each Student Book unit is dedicated to helping students develop numeracy skills they need for basic math work. In Unit 1, for example, students learn the numerals 1-10 and the English words for these numbers. Later in the book, students tackle activities like working with American money, reading Fahrenheit temperatures, and understanding numbers on a paycheck.

Civics and community involvement

Many institutions focus direct attention on the importance of civics instruction for English language learners. This type of instruction is often referred to as *EL/Civics*, and is designed to help students become active and informed community members. Lesson 9 in each Student Book unit explores a community-related topic. Labeled *In the Community*, these lessons have areas of focus like learning about garage sales, having a potluck dinner, using an ATM, and learning about health insurance.

Classes with literacy <u>and</u> low beginning students

A special *Taking Off* Literacy Workbook has been designed for literacy students enrolled in low beginning classes. Most low beginning students are true beginners in English who are literate in their first language. Literacy students, on the other hand, usually do not have fundamental first-language literacy skills. Literacy students often need specific instruction in letter formation and other fundamental reading, listening, and writing skills.

As teachers who have worked with mixed groups of literacy and low beginning students know, dealing simultaneously with the needs of each of these groups of learners is a great challenge. The Literacy Workbook offers a unique resource for teachers in such multi-level classes. Each Literacy Workbook unit provides essential support for key elements of the *Taking Off* Student Book. Working with or without a teacher's aide, literacy students can tackle basic reading, listening, and writing activities in the Literacy Workbook while their low beginning classmates tackle tasks at their ability level.

Scope and Sequence

Unit	Topics	Listening & Speaking Skills	Reading& Writing Skills
1 **Welcome to the classroom** *Page 2*	• Meeting new people • Alphabet • Greetings • Countries • Classroom language • Classroom objects • Emergency information form • Learning log	• Introduce yourself • Say the name of the country you come from • Listen and identify classroom objects • Say your telephone number, address, and email address • Ask for the spelling of words • Listen to and practice simple dialogs • Follow classroom directions	• Read and write alphabet letters • Interpret basic sight words • Write proper names, countries, and classroom words • Examine classroom commands/directions • Write and read personal information • Write new vocabulary in a learning log
2 **Where are you from?** *Page 14*	• Native language • Country of origin • Marriage • Physical appearance • Address • Identification form	• Collect information from classmates • Say the name of the country you come from • Say the language you speak • Recognize differences in marital status • Discuss hair and eye color	• Fill in information on a chart • Write personal information statements • Use writing to describe height • Identify vocabulary that describes physical appearance • Read and write words for select countries and languages
3 **This is my family.** *Page 26*	• Relatives • Name titles (Mr., Mrs., Ms.) • Family tree • Photo album • Ages • Census	• Ask questions about family • Discuss family members with classmates • Ask about someone's age • Listen to information about a census • Say name titles (Mr., Mrs., Ms.) • Recognize numbers 20-100	• Write family position words to complete a sentence • Read names using titles (Mr., Mrs., Ms.) • Make your own family tree • Examine classroom commands/directions • Read short sentences about a family • Complete a census form

Grammar Spotlight for Units 1-3

Page 38

• Pronouns (I, you, he, she, it, we, you, they)
• Present tense of BE in long form (I am) and short form (I'm)
• Present tense of BE with negatives (I'm not)
• Present tense of HAVE (I have/she has)

Review for Units 1-3

Page 40

• Matching activity: personal identification information
• Listening activity: marital status
• Community Challenge: find the address of the Registry/Department of Motor Vehicles

Numeracy	Community Awareness	EFF	SCANS	CASAS
• Learn numbers 1-10 • Identify numbers used in context • Say and write telephone numbers with area code • Say and write addresses and e-mail addresses • Understand page references	• Complete an emergency information form • Identify your emergency contact person • Learn 911 for police and fire emergencies	• Communicate so that others understand • Develop and maintain relationships with others • Learn new skills • Respect others and value diversity	• Basic skills (reading, speaking, writing, listening, arithmetic) • Analyzes and communicates information • Knowing how to learn	**1**: 0.1.1, 0.1.4 **3**: 0.2.1, 0.1.6 **8**: 6.0.1 **9**: 0.2.2, 2.1.2
• Learn numbers 11-19 • Say and write numbers in an address • Say and write zip codes	• Complete a detailed identification form • Learn to write your name as follows: last name, first name, middle initial • Learn the components of an address	• Listen to and learn from others' experiences and ideas • Learn new skills • Respect others and value diversity • Communicate so that others understand	• Basic skills (reading, speaking, writing, listening, arithmetic) • Works with people of diverse backgrounds • Sociability	**1, 2, 3**: 0.1.2, 0.2.1, 2.7.2. **5**: 1.1.4 **8**: 6.0.1
• Learn numbers 20-100 • Say your age • Recognize number words • Write the number of family members in your household • Write the ages of family members	• Learn about the American census • Complete a census form for your family	• Find and use community resources and services • Develop a sense of self that reflects your history, values, beliefs and roles in the larger community • Recognize and understand your civic responsibilities	• Basic skills (reading, speaking, writing, listening, arithmetic) • Seeing things in the mind's eye	**2, 6**: 7.4.8 **8**: 6.0.2 **9**: 0.2.2 **GS**: 1.9.2

CASAS Standards: Numbers in bold indicate lesson numbers.
GS: Grammar Spotlight

Scope and Sequence

Unit	Topics	Listening & Speaking Skills	Reading& Writing Skills
4 **Welcome to our house** *Page 42*	• Rooms in a house • Items in a house • Types of houses • Household needs • Your dream house • Garage sales	• Listen to and recognize the rooms in a house • Discuss household items • Learn the names of different types of housing • Speak with a partner about household needs • Differentiate between numbers that sound alike (18 vs. 80)	• Write the names of the rooms in a house • Review a paragraph about a new apartment • Write and read about a dream house • Read a paragraph about garage sales
5 **I play soccer on Saturday.** *Page 54*	• Daily activities • Days of the week • Months and dates • Time • Movies • Appointments • Medical history form	• Discuss your daily activities • Say the days of the week • Say the months in a year • Talk about movie times • Use the telephone to make appointments • Listen to ordinal numbers	• Read the time on clocks and watches • Complete a calendar for the week • Recognize abbreviations for months • Write times on a calendar • Read information about study times • Write and read ordinal numbers • Complete a medical history form
6 **Let's go shopping.** *Page 66*	• Clothes • Colors • Clothing sizes • Money • Paying by check	• Listen to and identify articles of clothing • Ask for what you need in a store • Ask about clothing size • Say that clothing is too large or small • Say color words • Ask about favorite colors	• Read and write clothing words • Complete a chart about clothing sizes • Write sentences about your clothing size • Learn words for American coins and bills

Grammar Spotlight for Units 4-6 *Page 78*	• Singular and Plural Nouns Ending in *-ch, -sh, -s,* and *-x* • A/an (a house/an apartment) • Simple present tense of regular verbs

Review for Units 4-6 *Page 80*	• Matching activity: housing, clothing, and time information • Writing sentences about new furniture • Community Challenge: interpret a check-out page on an Internet shopping site

Numeracy	Community Awareness	EFF	SCANS	CASAS
• Differentiate between numbers with similar digits • Complete sentences using numbers • Understand page references	• Learn that garage sales are community activities • Recognize the different types of houses in a community	• Provide for physical needs • Get involved in the community and get others involved • Reflect on and reevaluate your opinions and ideas	• Basic skills (reading, speaking, writing, listening, arithmetic) • Responsibility • Knowing how to learn • Creative thinking	**1, 4**: 1.4.1 **7**: 7.1.1 **9**: 1.1.6, 1.3.1, 2.6.1 2.7.2
• Practice ordinal numbers • Recognize the days and dates on a calendar • Say the time a movie begins • Write your date of birth on a form	• Complete a health clinic information form • Learn about the following services: dental cleaning, car tune-up, and haircut • Keep community appointments on a calendar	• Recognize and understand your human and civic responsibilities • Manage time and resources	• Basic skills (reading, speaking, writing, listening, arithmetic) • Analyzes and communicates information • Uses time wisely	**1**: 0.2.4 **2, 3**: 2.3.2 **4**: 2.3.1 **6**: 2.1.8, 7.1.4 **7**: 7.1.4 **8**: 0.2.1, 6.0.1 **9**: 3.2.1
• Write a check • Recognize American coin and bill denominations • Match coins and bills to monetary values	• Shop at a department store • Buy clothes in a store • Recognize and use American money	• Participate in group processes and decision making • Figure out how economic systems work • Use technology and work tools	• Basic skills (reading, speaking, writing, listening, arithmetic) • Use technology to complete results • Problem solving	**1**: 0.1.3, 1.3.9 **3**: 8.1.2 **5**: 7.5.1 **6**: 1.1.9, 1.2.1 **7**: 1.2.2 **8**: 1.1.6, 6.0.2 **9**: 1.8.2

CASAS Standards: Numbers in bold indicate lesson numbers.

Scope and Sequence

Unit	Topics	Listening & Speaking Skills	Reading & Writing Skills
7 **I'm so hungry!** *Page 82*	• Grocery shopping • Food • Food groups • Containers for food • Meals • Potluck dinner	• Listen for the names of food items • Talk about a shopping list • Discuss breakfast, lunch, and dinner foods • Order in a restaurant • Ask and answer questions about foods you eat	• Make a shopping list • Read the names of food items • Complete a chart about location of foods in a supermarket • Read a paragraph about pot luck dinners
8 **How's the weather?** *Page 94*	• Weather • Seasons • Leisure activities • Temperature (Fahrenheit) • U.S. map	• Discuss different types of weather • Listen to and discuss leisure activities • Discuss activities you like to do in different seasons • Talk about temperature in a city	• Read and write about the seasons • Recognize weather-related vocabulary • Write sentences about weather • Interpret a weather map
9 **Where's the post office?** *Page 106*	• Neighborhood map • Places in the community • Banking • ATM (Automated Teller Machine)	• Talk about places you see in your neighborhood • Ask and answer questions about the location of neighborhood places • Ask your classmates what places they live near • Ask your partner where they do things	• Read a neighborhood map • Write sentences about the location of neighborhood places • Read about depositing money into a savings account • Read about how to use an ATM

Grammar Spotlight for Units 7-9 *Page 118*	• Present continuous (I am/I'm working) • Question words (where, how, what)

Review for Units 7-9 *Page 120*	• Matching activity: weather, seasons, and community-related information • Listening activity: weather, seasons, and leisure activities • Community Challenge: find addresses for community places (post office)

Numeracy	Community Awareness	EFF	SCANS	CASAS
• Write times of the day for meals • Use times of the day in sentences • Use container words to talk about food (a bunch of grapes)	• Explore a supermarket • Learn about a potluck dinner • Practice ordering food in a restaurant	• Provide for physical needs • Listen to and learn from others experiences and ideas • Get involved in community and get others involved	• Basic skills (reading, speaking, writing, listening, arithmetic) • Sociability • Understands how systems work • Analyzes and communicates information • Self-management	**1**: 7.1.2 **2**: 1.3.8 **3**: 1.3.7 **4**: 3.5.2 **5**: 8.2.1 **6**: 2.6.4 **7**: 3.5.9 **8**: 1.1.4 **9**: 2.7.2 **R**: 7.4.3
• Interpret a thermometer in degrees Fahrenheit • Write numbers using degrees Fahrenheit	• Read a weather map • Talk about the weather in your community • Discuss community-related leisure activities	• Find, interpret and analyze diverse sources of information • Listen to and learn from others' experiences and ideas • Reflect on and reevaluate your opinions and ideas	• Basic skills (reading, speaking, writing, listening, arithmetic) • Decision making • Reasoning • Seeing things in the mind's eye	**1**: 2.3.3, 5.7.3 **2**: 1.1.5 **6**: 0.2.4 **8**: 1.1.5 **9**: 1.1.3, 2.3.3 **R**: 7.4.2
• Read dates and money amounts on a bank deposit slip • Discuss a deposit slip • Complete a bank withdrawal • Use an ATM PIN number	• Interpret a neighborhood map • Recognize businesses in your community • Practice banking procedures	• Get involved in the community and get others involved • Find, interpret, and analyze diverse sources of information • Use technology and other work tools • Find and use community resources and services	• Basic skills (reading, speaking, writing, listening, arithmetic) • Seeing things in the mind's eyes • Understands how systems work • Uses technology to complete tasks • Acquires and evaluates information	**2**: 2.2.1, 2.2.5 **3**: 2.5.4 **7**: 0.2.4 **8**: 1.8.2 **9**: 1.8.1 **GS**: 2.1.1, 2.5.1, 2.5.5

CASAS Standards: Numbers in bold indicate lesson numbers.
R: Review
GS: Grammar Spotlight

Scope and Sequence

Unit	Topics	Listening & Speaking Skills	Reading& Writing Skills
10 **You need to see a doctor.** *Page 122*	• Health problems • Medicine • Healthy food • Exercise • Health insurance	• Listen and respond to dialogs about illness • Express physical pain • Make a doctor's appointment for your child • Discuss medicines and remedies • Listen to information about health insurance • Follow TPR (Total Physical Response) directions	• Recognize words for physical ailments • Chart health problems and remedies • Read about staying fit and healthy • Interpret a health insurance card
11 **What's your job?** *Page 134*	• Jobs • Workplaces • Driving • Want ads • Paycheck • Job application	• Talk about jobs • Say what job conditions you like (indoors, with people) • Say what work-related skills you can do (fix things) • Ask and answer questions with affirmative and negative responses	• Examine the tools different jobs require • Complete sentences about what you and others can do • Read want ads • Fill in a form about what your job was before • Complete sentences about paychecks • Practice with a job application
12 **How do you get to class?** *Page 146*	• Transportation • Directions to places in the community • Learner's permit • Road signs • Bus schedule	• Practice dialogs about methods of transportation • Differentiate among left, right, and straight ahead • Follow directions in the community • Listen to dialogs about time phrases • Ask when the next bus or train leaves	• Use a community map to give directions • Analyze a bus schedule • Complete sentences about a learner's permit • Read and respond to road signs
Grammar Spotlight for Units 10-12 *Page 158*	• Can/can't (I, you, he, she, it, we, they) • Prepositions of place(in, on, next to, between)		
Review for Units 10-12 *Page 160*	• Matching activity: health, job, and transportation information • Listening activity: doctor's appointments • Community Challenge: interpret a bus schedule		

Numeracy	Community Awareness	EFF	SCANS	CASAS
• Learn about health insurance co-payments • Say medicine dosages	• Complete health insurance forms • Understand a doctor's role in the community • Read a medicine label from a community pharmacy	• Provide for physical needs • Provide a nurturing home environment • Pursue personal self-improvement • Figure out how social service systems work	• Basic skills (reading, speaking, writing, listening, arithmetic) • Acquires and evaluates information • Problem solving • Self-management • Works within the system	**1, 2**: 3.1.1 **3**: 3.1.3 **4**: 3.3.1 **6, 7**: 3.5.9 **8**: 3.3.2 **9**: 3.2.3 **R**: 8.3.1
• Understand paycheck deductions • Learn about hourly wages • Review concept of depositing money in bank account	• Examine various jobs in the community • Recognize want ads as a community resource • Gain information about the job application process • Complete an employment application form	• Find and get a job • Meet new work challenges • Plan and renew career goals • Figure out how economic systems work • Balance and support work, career, and personal goals	• Basic skills (reading, speaking, writing, listening, arithmetic) • Use personnel resources • Understands how systems work • Reasoning • Self-esteem	**1**: 4.1.6 **2**: 4.1.8 **3**: 7.5.1 **5**: 4.4.2 **6**: 4.1.3 **7**: 4.1.2 **8**: 4.2.1 **R**: 4.1.3
• Read times related to public transportation • Practice time phrases • Write month, date, and year in numerical form (MM/DD/YY)	• Read schedule for community transportation • Review various forms of transportation (bus, train, subway) • Get around your community	• Identify and monitor problems, community needs, strengths and resources • Manage time and resources • Figure out how systems work	• Basic skills (reading, speaking, writing, listening, arithmetic) • Knowing how to learn • Self-management • Understands how systems work • Creative thinking	**1**: 2.2.3 **2, 3**: 2.2.1 **4**: 0.1.2 **5**: 2.2.4 **6**: 1.9.2, 2.5.7 **7**: 1.9.1, 2.2.2 **8**: 6.6.6 **9**: 2.2.4 **GS**: 2.6.3

CASAS Standards: Numbers in bold indicate lesson numbers.
R: Review
GS: Grammar Spotlight

Guide to Taking Off

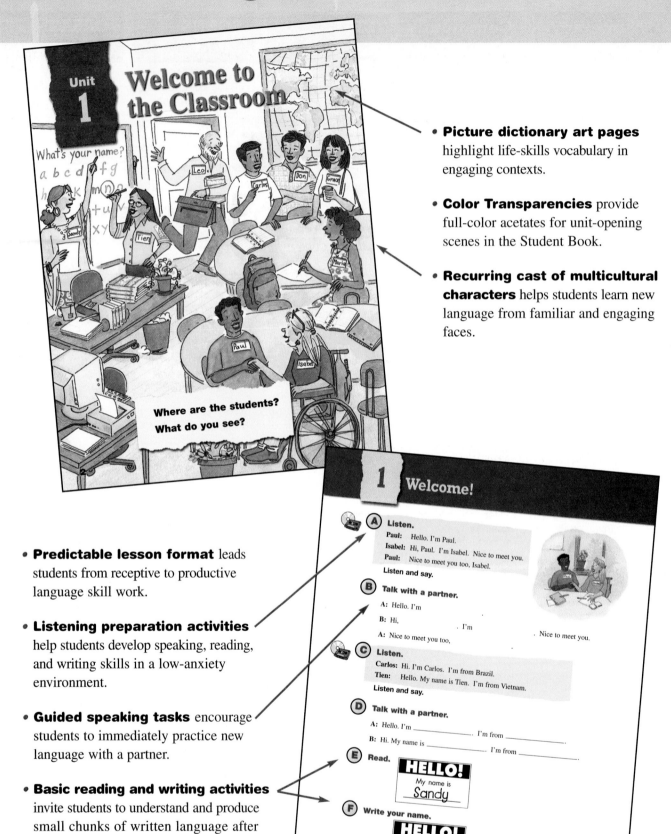

- **Picture dictionary art pages** highlight life-skills vocabulary in engaging contexts.

- **Color Transparencies** provide full-color acetates for unit-opening scenes in the Student Book.

- **Recurring cast of multicultural characters** helps students learn new language from familiar and engaging faces.

- **Predictable lesson format** leads students from receptive to productive language skill work.

- **Listening preparation activities** help students develop speaking, reading, and writing skills in a low-anxiety environment.

- **Guided speaking tasks** encourage students to immediately practice new language with a partner.

- **Basic reading and writing activities** invite students to understand and produce small chunks of written language after completing listening and speaking tasks.

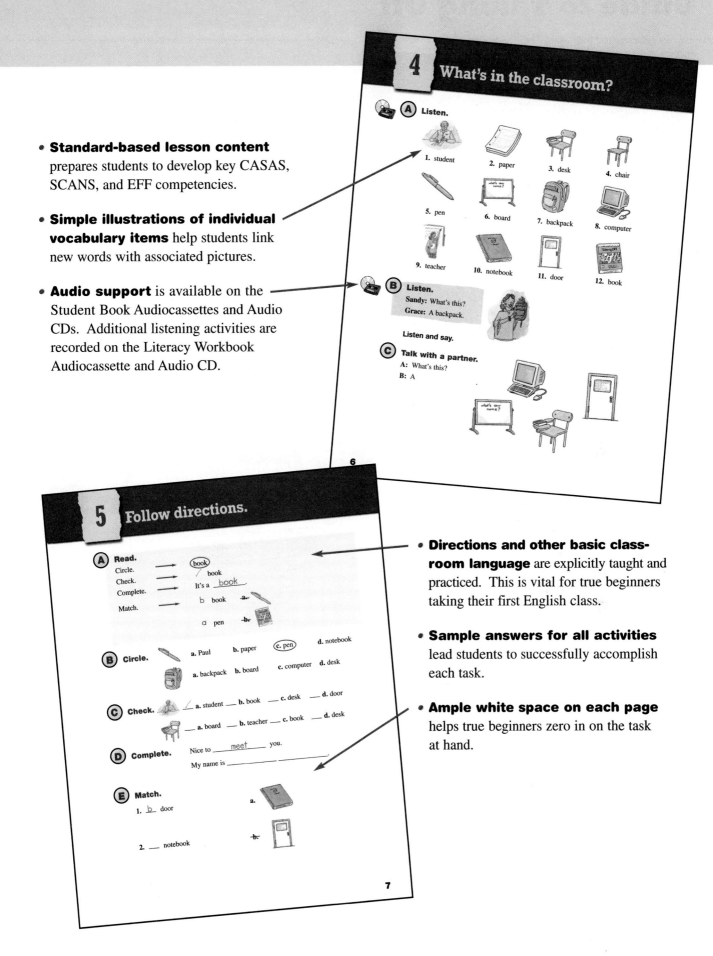

- **Standard-based lesson content** prepares students to develop key CASAS, SCANS, and EFF competencies.

- **Simple illustrations of individual vocabulary items** help students link new words with associated pictures.

- **Audio support** is available on the Student Book Audiocassettes and Audio CDs. Additional listening activities are recorded on the Literacy Workbook Audiocassette and Audio CD.

- **Directions and other basic class-room language** are explicitly taught and practiced. This is vital for true beginners taking their first English class.

- **Sample answers for all activities** lead students to successfully accomplish each task.

- **Ample white space on each page** helps true beginners zero in on the task at hand.

Guide to Taking Off

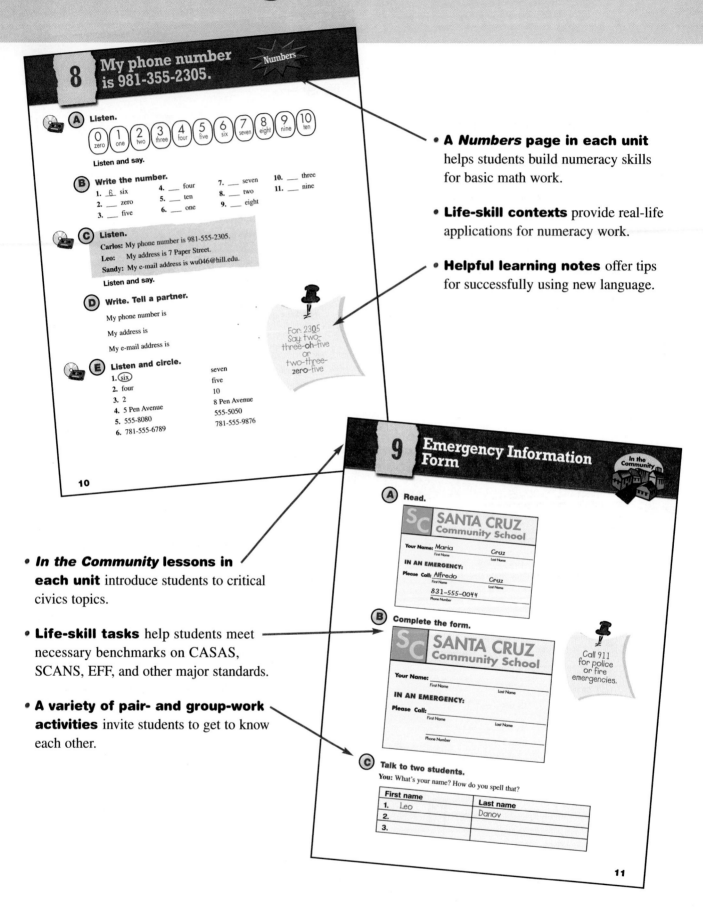

8 My phone number is 981-355-2305. *Numbers*

A Listen.
0 zero 1 one 2 two 3 three 4 four 5 five 6 six 7 seven 8 eight 9 nine 10 ten

Listen and say.

B Write the number.
1. 6 six
2. ___ zero
3. ___ five
4. ___ four
5. ___ ten
6. ___ one
7. ___ seven
8. ___ two
9. ___ eight
10. ___ three
11. ___ nine

C Listen.
Carlos: My phone number is 981-555-2305.
Leo: My address is 7 Paper Street.
Sandy: My e-mail address is wu046@hill.edu.

Listen and say.

D Write. Tell a partner.
My phone number is
My address is
My e-mail address is

E Listen and circle.
1. six / seven
2. four / five
3. 2 / 10
4. 5 Pen Avenue / 8 Pen Avenue
5. 555-8080 / 555-5050
6. 781-555-6789 / 781-555-9876

For: 2305
Say: two-three-oh-five
or
two-three-zero-five

10

- A *Numbers* page in each unit helps students build numeracy skills for basic math work.

- **Life-skill contexts** provide real-life applications for numeracy work.

- **Helpful learning notes** offer tips for successfully using new language.

9 Emergency Information Form *In the Community*

A Read.

SC SANTA CRUZ Community School
Your Name: Maria
First Name
Cruz
Last Name
IN AN EMERGENCY:
Please Call: Alfredo
First Name
Cruz
Last Name
831-555-0044
Phone Number

B Complete the form.

SC SANTA CRUZ Community School
Your Name:
First Name
Last Name
IN AN EMERGENCY:
Please Call:
First Name
Last Name
Phone Number

Call 911 for police or fire emergencies.

C Talk to two students.
You: What's your name? How do you spell that?

First name	Last name
1. Leo	Danov
2.	
3.	

11

- *In the Community* **lessons in each unit** introduce students to critical civics topics.

- **Life-skill tasks** help students meet necessary benchmarks on CASAS, SCANS, EFF, and other major standards.

- **A variety of pair- and group-work activities** invite students to get to know each other.

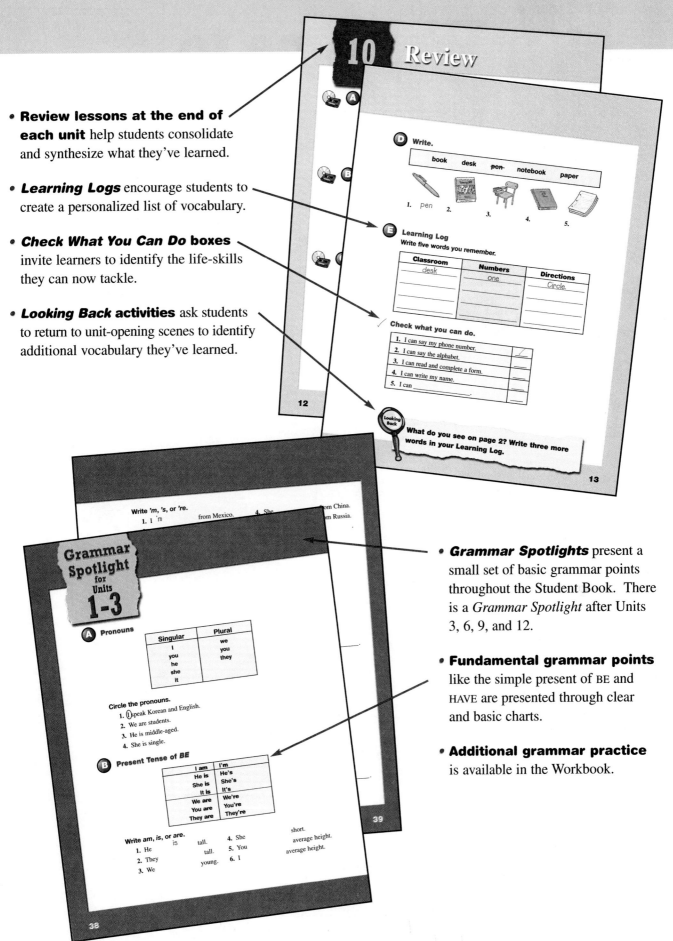

- **Review lessons at the end of each unit** help students consolidate and synthesize what they've learned.

- *Learning Logs* encourage students to create a personalized list of vocabulary.

- *Check What You Can Do* boxes invite learners to identify the life-skills they can now tackle.

- *Looking Back* activities ask students to return to unit-opening scenes to identify additional vocabulary they've learned.

- *Grammar Spotlights* present a small set of basic grammar points throughout the Student Book. There is a *Grammar Spotlight* after Units 3, 6, 9, and 12.

- **Fundamental grammar points** like the simple present of BE and HAVE are presented through clear and basic charts.

- **Additional grammar practice** is available in the Workbook.

Unit 1

Welcome to the Classroom

Where are the students?

What do you see?

A **Listen.**

Paul: Hello. I'm Paul.

Isabel: Hi, Paul. I'm Isabel. Nice to meet you.

Paul: Nice to meet you too, Isabel.

Listen and say.

B **Talk with a partner.**

A: Hello. I'm _____.

B: Hi, _____. I'm _____. Nice to meet you.

A: Nice to meet you too, _____.

C **Listen.**

Carlos: Hi. I'm Carlos. I'm from Brazil.

Tien: Hello. My name is Tien. I'm from Vietnam.

Listen and say.

D **Talk with a partner.**

A: Hi. I'm _____. I'm from _____.

B: Hello. My name is _____. I'm from _____.

E **Read.**

F **Write your name.**

3

A **Listen.**

(Aa) (Bb) (Cc) (Dd) (Ee) (Ff) (Gg) (Hh) (Ii) (Jj) (Kk) (Ll) (Mm)

(Nn) (Oo) (Pp) (Qq) (Rr) (Ss) (Tt) (Uu) (Vv) (Ww) (Xx) (Yy) (Zz)

Listen and say.

B **Write.**

A	B	C	D	E	F	G	H	I	J	K	L	M
A	___	___	___	___	___	___	___	___	___	___	___	___

a	b	c	d	e	f	g	h	i	j	k	l	m
a	___	___	___	___	___	___	___	___	___	___	___	___

C **Write.**

N	O	P	Q	R	S	T	U	V	W	X	Y	Z
___	___	___	___	___	___	___	___	___	___	___	___	___

n	o	p	q	r	s	t	u	v	w	x	y	z
___	___	___	___	___	___	___	___	___	___	___	___	___

  D **Listen and say the letters.**

1. U S A
2. J A P A N
3. B R A Z I L
4. M E X I C O

5. V I E T N A M
6. T H A I L A N D
7. C O L O M B I A
8. V E N E Z U E L A

  E **Listen and write.**

1. n a m e
2. ___ ___ ___ ___ ___
3. ___ ___ ___ ___

4. ___ ___ ___ ___ ___
5. ___ ___ ___

4

A Listen.

Maria: I'm Maria Cruz. What's your name?

Tien: My name is Tien Lam.

Maria: How do you spell that?

Tien: My first name is T-I-E-N. My last name is L-A-M.

Listen and say.

B Talk with a partner.

A: Hello. I'm _____ _____. What's your name?

B: My name is _____ _____.

A: How do you spell that?

B: My first name is __ __ __ __ __ __. My last name is __ __ __ __ __ __.

C Play *Alphabet Bingo.*

Write letters of the alphabet.

Listen to your teacher.

A Listen.

1. student

2. paper

3. desk

4. chair

5. pen

6. board

7. backpack

8. computer

9. teacher

10. notebook

11. door

12. book

B Listen.

Sandy: What's this?

Grace: A backpack.

Listen and say.

C Talk with a partner.

A: What's this?

B: A _____.

A Read.

Circle.   ⟶   (book)

Check.   ⟶   ✓ book

Complete.   ⟶   It's a __book__.

Match.   ⟶

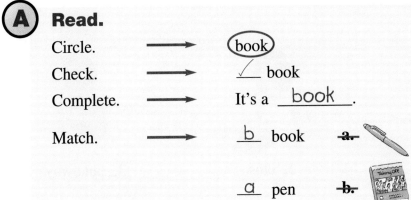

    _b_ book   ~~a.~~

    _a_ pen   ~~b.~~

B Circle.

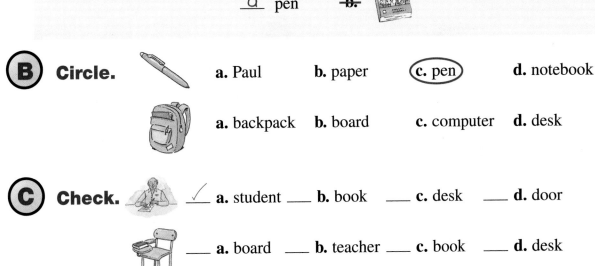

a. Paul   b. paper   (c. pen)   d. notebook

a. backpack   b. board   c. computer   d. desk

C Check.

✓ a. student   __ b. book   __ c. desk   __ d. door

__ a. board   __ b. teacher   __ c. book   __ d. desk

D Complete.

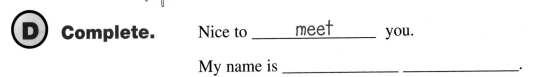

Nice to __meet__ you.

My name is _____ _____.

E Match.

1. _b_ door   a.

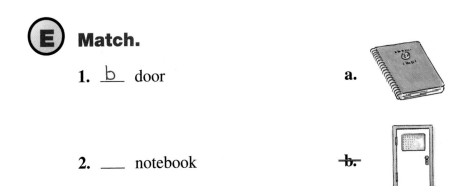

2. __ notebook   ~~b.~~

7

A Listen.

1. open

2. close

3. put away

4. go to

5. take out

6. point to

Listen and say.

B Listen and circle.

1.

2.

3.

(A) Listen. ✓ Check what you hear.

1. ___ Close the door. ✓ Open the door.
2. ___ Go to the board. ___ Point to the board.
3. ___ Take out the pen. ___ Put away the pen.
4. ___ Put away the notebook. ___ Point to the notebook.
5. ___ Close the door. ___ Open the door.
6. ___ Take out the paper. ___ Put away the paper.
7. ___ Point to the desk. ___ Go to the desk.
8. ___ Open the book. ___ Take out the book.

(B) Complete. Tell a partner.

1. Open the ___door___. 4. Go to the _____.
2. Take out the _____. 5. Put away the _____.
3. Close the _____. 6. Point to the _____.

(C) Play *Follow the Leader.*

Complete.

1. Open the ___book___.
2. Take out the _____.
3. Close the _____.
4. Go to the _____.
5. Put away the _____.
6. Point to the _____.

Tell your classmates.

Point to the door.

A **Listen.**

0 zero	1 one	2 two	3 three	4 four	5 five	6 six	7 seven	8 eight	9 nine	10 ten

Listen and say.

B **Write the number.**

1. _6_ six   4. ___ four   7. ___ seven   10. ___ three

2. ___ zero   5. ___ ten   8. ___ two   11. ___ nine

3. ___ five   6. ___ one   9. ___ eight

C **Listen.**

Carlos: My phone number is 981-555-2305.

Leo: My address is 7 Paper Street.

Sandy: My e-mail address is wu046@hill.edu.

Listen and say.

D **Write. Tell a partner.**

My phone number is _____.

My address is _____.

My e-mail address is _____.

For: 2305
Say: two-
three-**oh**-five
or
two-three-
zero-five

E **Listen and circle.**

1. (six)   seven

2. four   five

3. 2   10

4. 5 Pen Avenue   8 Pen Avenue

5. 555-8080   555-5050

6. 781-555-6789   781-555-9876

10

Emergency Information Form

A Read.

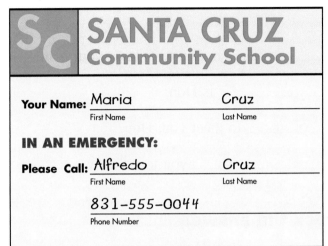

SC SANTA CRUZ Community School

Your Name: Maria   Cruz
First Name   Last Name

IN AN EMERGENCY:

Please Call: Alfredo   Cruz
First Name   Last Name

831-555-0044
Phone Number

B Complete the form.

SC SANTA CRUZ Community School

Your Name: _____
First Name   Last Name

IN AN EMERGENCY:

Please Call: _____
First Name   Last Name

_____
Phone Number

Call 911 for police or fire emergencies.

C Talk to two students.

You: What's your name? How do you spell that?

First name	Last name
1. Leo	Danov
2.	
3.	

10 Review

A Listen and write.

Sandy: _____Hi_____. I'm Sandy. What's your name?

Don: My _____ is Don.

Sandy: _____ to meet you, Don.

Don: Nice to _____ you too, Sandy.

B Listen and ✓ check the answer.

1. ___ 7 Paper Street.   ✓ Don.
2. ___ Nice to meet you, too.   ___ Go to the board.
3. ___ Isabel.   ___ Ten.
4. ___ I-S-A-B-E-L.   ___ Book.
5. ___ Three.   ___ A chair.
6. ___ 310-555-0123.   ___ 2039 Door Street.

C Listen and write.

first	how	I'm	last	name

Sandy: Hi. _____ Sandy. What's your name?

Grace: My _____ is Grace Lee.

Sandy: _____ do you spell that?

Grace: My _____ name is G-R-A-C-E.

My _____ name is L-E-E.

D **Write.**

book	desk	~~pen~~	notebook	paper

1. _pen_   2. _____   3. _____   4. _____   5. _____

E **Learning Log**

Write five words you remember.

Classroom	Numbers	Directions
desk	one	Circle.

✓ **Check what you can do.**

1. I can say my phone number.	✓
2. I can say the alphabet.	___
3. I can read and complete a form.	___
4. I can write my name.	___
5. I can _____.	___

What do you see on page 2? Write three more words in your Learning Log.

Unit 2 — Where are you from?

Where are the students?

What do you see?

A Listen.

Leo: I'm from Russia. Where are you from?

Don: I'm from Korea.

Listen and say.

B Talk with a partner.

A: I'm from _____. Where are you from?

B: I'm from _____.

C Listen.

Grace: Where is Carlos from?

Maria: He's from Brazil.

Grace: Where is Isabel from?

Maria: She's from Colombia.

Listen and say.

D Talk with classmates.

A: Where is _____ from?

B: He's | from _____.
She's |

WORD LIST

Grace/China
Leo/Russia
Don/Korea
Maria/Mexico

A Listen.

Isabel: I speak Spanish.
What language do you speak?

Carlos: I speak Portuguese.

Listen and say.

B Talk with a partner.

A: I speak _____. What language do you speak?

B: I speak _____.

C Talk with three classmates. Complete the chart.

What's your name?	Where are you from?	What language do you speak?
Grace	China	Chinese
1.		
2.		
3.		

D Write.

My name is _____.

I'm from _____. I speak _____.

16

A Read. Complete the chart.

Carlos

Don

Tien

Maria

Name	Country	Language
Carlos	Brazil	Portuguese
Don	Korea	Korean
Tien	Vietnam	Vietnamese
Maria	Mexico	Spanish
You	_____	_____

B Listen.

Paul: Carlos is from Brazil. What language does he speak?

Grace: He speaks Portuguese.

Paul: Tien is from Vietnam. What language does she speak?

Grace: She speaks Vietnamese.

Listen and say.

C Talk with classmates about Carlos, Don, Tien, and Maria.

A: _____ is from _____. What language does _____ speak?
                                                                  (he/she)

B: _____ speaks _____.
     (He/She)

17

A Listen.

1. married

2. single

3. divorced

4. widowed

Listen and say.

B Listen and circle.

1.

2.

3.

18

A **Listen.**

Leo   Paul   Carlos   Don   Tien

Paul: I am **average height**.

Leo is **tall**.

Tien is **short**.

Don and Carlos are **average height**.

Listen and say.

B **Talk with a partner.**

Tien and Maria are _____.

Grace is _____.

Sandy is _____ height.

Tien   Maria   Sandy   Grace

C **Write about three classmates.**

Leo is tall.

1. _____ is _____.

2. _____ is _____.

3. _____ is _____.

19

A Listen.

Leo has green eyes.

Isabel has blue eyes.

Leo and Isabel don't wear glasses.

Tien has brown eyes. She wears glasses.

Listen and say.

B Talk to a partner.

I have _____ eyes. I _____ glasses.

(wear/ don't wear)

C Listen.

Sandy: I have red hair.

Paul and Tien have brown hair.

Leo has white hair.

Isabel has blond hair.

Listen and say.

D Complete the sentence.

I have _____ hair.

E Write about three classmates.

1. _____ has _____ hair.

2. _____ has _____ eyes.

3. _____ wears glasses.

A Match.

1. _d_ glasses   **a.**

2. ___ married   **b.**

3. ___ brown hair   **c.**

4. ___ green eyes   ~~**d.**~~

B Listen. Write the number.

 ___ Maria

 ___ Grace

 ___ Isabel

 ___ Sandy

 ___ Leo

 _1_ Carlos

A Listen.

| 11 eleven | 12 twelve | 13 thirteen | 14 fourteen | 15 fifteen | 16 sixteen | 17 seventeen | 18 eighteen | 19 nineteen |

Listen and say.

B Write the numbers.

__11__   _____   _____   14   _____   16   _____   _____   __19__

C Write the number.

1. __11__ eleven   3. ___ seventeen   5. ___ twelve   7. ___ fifteen

2. ___ sixteen   4. ___ thirteen   6. ___ eighteen   8. ___ fourteen

D Listen.

Don: What's your address?

Paul: My address is 1714 Brown Street.

Don: What's your zip code?

Paul: My zip code is 01313.

Listen and say.

E Complete. Talk with a partner.

My address is _____.   My zip code is _____.

Identification Form

A Read.

IDENTIFICATION FORM

TYPE OR PRINT

Danov	Leo	V.
LAST NAME	FIRST NAME	MI

17 White Street	Los Angeles	CA	90011
ADDRESS	CITY	STATE	ZIP

CIRCLE ONE:

MARITAL STATUS: SINGLE   MARRIED   (DIVORCED)   WIDOWED

EYE COLOR: BLUE   BROWN   (GREEN)   BLACK

HAIR COLOR: BROWN   BLACK   (WHITE)   RED   BLOND

B Complete the form.

IDENTIFICATION FORM

TYPE OR PRINT

LAST NAME	FIRST NAME	MI

ADDRESS	CITY	STATE	ZIP

CIRCLE ONE:

MARITAL STATUS: SINGLE   MARRIED   DIVORCED   WIDOWED

EYE COLOR: BLUE   BROWN   GREEN   BLACK

HAIR COLOR: BROWN   BLACK   WHITE   RED   BLOND

10 Review

A Listen and write.

Grace: I am _____tall_____.

Leo: I _____ Russian.

Tien: I wear _____.

Isabel: I have _____ hair. I have _____ eyes.

B Listen and ✓ check.

1. ____ I'm from Vietnam.   ✓ I speak Vietnamese.
2. ____ Leo is divorced.   ____ Sandy has red hair.
3. ____ Korea.   ____ Korean.
4. ____ 02090.   ____ San Diego, California.

C Play *Guess Who!*

Write about a classmate. Read your sentences to the class. Say, "Guess who!"

1. _____ has _____ eyes.
   (He/She)

2. _____ has _____ hair.
   (He/She)

3. _____ (wears/doesn't wear) glasses.
   (He/She)

Guess who!

Write. Complete the sentences.

red	blue	brown	green	wears

1. Pete has _____ eyes.
2. Pete has _____ hair.
3. Linda has _____ hair.
4. Linda has _____ eyes.
5. Linda _____ glasses.

E **Learning Log**

Write five words you remember.

Countries	Colors	Numbers
Brazil	green	twelve

✓ **Check what you can do.**

1. I can say my hair and eye color.	____
2. I can ask people where they are from.	____
3. I can write my country's name.	____
4. I can say my country and language.	____
5. I can _____.	____

Looking Back

What do you see on page 14? Write three more words in your Learning Log.

This is my family.

**Who do you see
on this page?**

A **Listen.**

1. mother

2. father

3. brother

4. husband

5. daughter

6. sons

Listen and say.

  B **Listen.**

Julia: What's your father's name?

Sandy: His name is Arthur. And your father's name?

Julia: His name is Mark.

Listen and say.

 C **Talk with a partner.**

A: What's your _____'s name?

B: His name is _____.

And your _____'s name?

A: His name is _____.

WORD LIST

brother
father
son

A **Listen.**

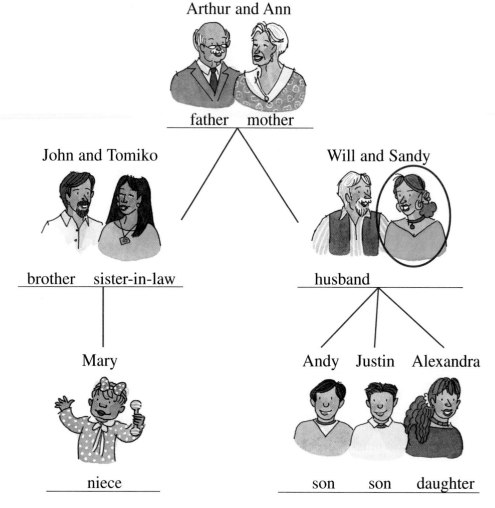

Arthur and Ann

father mother

John and Tomiko

brother sister-in-law

Will and Sandy

husband

Mary

niece

Andy Justin Alexandra

son son daughter

Listen and say.

  B **Listen and write.**

1. Justin is Sandy's ____son____.

2. Alexandra is Sandy's _____.

3. John is Sandy's _____.

4. Will is Sandy's _____.

5. Arthur is Sandy's _____.

6. Ann is Sandy's _____.

7. Tomiko is Sandy's _____.

8. Mary is Sandy's _____.

A **Listen.**

Isabel: Who is Arthur?

Don: Arthur is Sandy's father.

Listen and say.

B **Talk with a partner. Look at the pictures on page 28.**

A: Who is _____?
         (name)

B: _____ is Sandy's _____. Who is _____?
   (name)   (name)

A: _____ is Sandy's _____.
   (name)

C **Work with classmates. Read and circle.**

1. **Who is Will?**
   a. Sandy's brother
   b. Sandy's husband

2. **Who is Mary?**
   a. Sandy's daughter
   b. Sandy's niece

3. **Who is John?**
   a. Sandy's brother
   b. Sandy's father

4. **Who is Arthur?**
   a. Sandy's brother
   b. Sandy's father

5. **Who are Andy and Justin?**
   a. Sandy's sons
   b. Sandy's brothers

6. **Who is Tomiko?**
   a. Sandy's daughter
   b. Sandy's sister-in-law

A **Listen.**

Paul: Do you have children?

Leo: Yes, I have three daughters.

Tien: No, I don't.

Listen and say.

 B **Talk with a partner.**

A: Do you have children?

B: | Yes, I have _____.
       | No, I don't.

  C **Listen.**

Tien: Do you have two brothers?

Carlos: Yes, I do.

Tien: Please sign here.

Carlos: Do you have a daughter?

Tien: No, I don't.

Listen and say.

 D **Ask classmates. Complete the chart.**

You: Do you have two brothers?

Carlos: Yes, I do.

You: Please sign here.

a son	two children	a daughter
name: _____	name: _____	name: _____
a brother	two daughters	two brothers
name: _____	name: _____	name: _____Carlos

A Listen.

1. Mr. and Mrs. Hancock **2.** Mr. Hancock and Ms. Tanaka **3.** Ms. Lopez

Listen and say.

B Work with a partner. Write *Mr.*, *Ms.*, or *Mrs.*

1. <u>Mrs.</u> Sandy Johnson

3. _____ Leo Danov

2. _____ Isabel Lopez

4. _____ Paul Lemat

A   Write. Complete Carlos's family tree.

Umberto and Vera

Relatives = people in your family

___grandfather___ ___grandmother___

Celina and Ricardo

Magda and Rudolfo

___aunt___   ___uncle___

_____ _____

Carlos   Alfredo   Lina

_____ ___sister___

B   Write about your family.

1. My father's name is _____.

2. My mother's name is _____.

3. My grandmother's name is _____.

4. My grandfather's name is _____.

5. My _____'s name is _____.

A Listen and read.

This is Don's family.

1. Don's grandfather is <u>old</u>.

2. His parents are <u>middle-aged</u>.

3. His aunt is <u>middle-aged</u>, too.

4. Sumin is his sister. She is <u>young</u>.

B Complete the sentences about Leo's family.

1.  Leo's mother is _____ old _____ .

2.  Leo's granddaughter is _____.

3.  Leo's sisters are _____.

A Listen.

20 twenty	**21** twenty-one	**22** twenty-two	**23** twenty-three	**24** twenty-four	**25** twenty-five
26 twenty-six	**27** twenty-seven	**28** twenty-eight	**29** twenty-nine	**30** thirty	**40** forty
50 fifty	**60** sixty	**70** seventy	**80** eighty	**90** ninety	**100** one hundred

Listen and say.

B Write the numbers.

1. _28_ twenty-eight   6. ____ forty

2. ____ thirty   7. ____ eighty

3. ____ ninety   8. ____ seventy

4. ____ sixty   9. ____ one hundred

5. ____ fifty   10. ____ forty-one

C Listen.

Grace: How old are you, Sumin?

Sumin: I'm ten years old.

Listen and say.

D Talk with a partner.

A: How old are you?

B: I'm _____.

34

  A **Listen and read.**

This is a census form. The census is a count of all the people in a country. Families in the U.S. complete a census.

Census Form

Address: _____2954 Short Street_____

_____Los Angeles_____ ___CA___ ___90002___
City   State   Zip Code

List all the people at your address

Mr./Mrs./Ms. First Name	MI	Last Name	Age
1. Mr. William	D.	Johnson	57
2. Mrs. Sandra	H.	Johnson	49
3. Mr. Andrew	H.	Johnson	17
4.			
5.			

B **Complete the form.**

Census Form

Address: _____

_____ _____ _____
City   State   Zip Code

List all the people at your address

Mr./Mrs./Ms. First Name	MI	Last Name	Age
1.			
2.			
3.			
4.			
5.			

10 Review

 A **Listen and write.**

1. My name is _____Ms._____ Redman.
2. I live at _____ Brown Road.
3. I am _____.
4. My husband's _____ is Bill.
5. We have five _____.
6. My _____ has five children, too.

B **Listen and ✓ check.**

1. ___ 92617.   ✓ 35.
2. ___ Yes, I have two sons.   ___ What about you?
3. ___ Yes, she is.   ___ Maria Cruz.
4. ___ 25 years old.   ___ Sandy's son.
5. ___ Sandy's grandfather.   ___ Sandy's mother.

C **Listen and circle.**

1. (80)	18	**5.** 70	17
2. 70	60	**6.** 20	12
3. 19	90	**7.** 14	45
4. 25	20	**8.** 15	50

D **Write *Mr.*, *Ms.*, or *Mrs.***

1. Sandy is married. She is _____Ms._____ or _____ Johnson.
2. Will is Sandy's husband. He is _____ Johnson.
3. Tien is single. She is _____ Lam.
4. Leo is a man. He is _____ Danov.

E **Complete the chart. Write about your family.**

Your Family	Name	Married, Single, Divorced, Widowed
mother		
father		
sister		
brother		

F **Learning Log**

Write five words you remember.

Relatives	Ages	Numbers
mother	young	twenty

✓ **Check what you can do.**

1. I can talk about my family.	_____
2. I can use *Mrs.*, *Ms.*, and *Mr.*	_____
3. I can read a family tree.	_____
4. I can say and write numbers from 1-100.	_____
5 I can _____.	_____

Looking Back

Who are the people on page 26? Write three more words in your Learning Log.

Grammar Spotlight
for Units 1-3

A  **Pronouns**

Singular	Plural
I	we
you	you
he	they
she	
it	

Circle the pronouns.

1. (I) speak Korean and English.

2. We are students.

3. He is middle-aged.

4. She is single.

B **Present Tense of BE**

	I am	I'm
	He is	He's
	She is	She's
	It is	It's
	We are	We're
	You are	You're
	They are	They're

Write am, is, or are.

1. He ____is____ tall.

2. They _____ tall.

3. We _____ young.

4. She _____ short.

5. You _____ average height.

6. I _____ average height.

Write 'm, 's, or 're.

1. I _'m_ from Mexico.

2. You _____ from Haiti.

3. They _____ from the U.S.

4. She _____ from China.

5. We _____ from Russia.

6. I _____ .

C BE with Negatives

I'm not	He's not She's not It's not	We're not You're not They're not

Write negative sentences.

1. Maria is widowed. _She's not_ married now.

2. Sandy and I are married. _____ single.

3. Carlos and Tien are single. _____ married.

4. _I'm not_____ .

D Present Tense of HAVE

I have You have He has She has It has	We have You have They have

Write have or has. Then write a sentence about you.

1. Tien and Paul _have_ brown eyes.

2. Carlos _____ brown eyes, too.

3. The three friends _____ black hair.

4. Will _____ blue eyes and white hair.

5. I _____ .

A **Match.**

1. _f_ What's your name?   **a.** 5 Young Avenue.

2. ___ How do you spell that?   **b.** C-A-R-L-O-S A-V-I-L-A.

3. ___ Where are you from?   **c.** 35670.

4. ___ What's your telephone number?   **d.** Portuguese.

5. ___ What's your address?   **e.** Brazil.

6. ___ What's your zip code?   **f.** Carlos Avila.

7. ___ What language do you speak?   **g.** 949-555-0000.

B **Listen and** ✓ **check.**

1. ✓ **a.**   ___ **b.**

2. ___ **a.**   ___ **b.**

3. ___ **a.**    ___ **b.**

Circle the words.

> ~~AVERAGE,~~ BACKPACK, DAUGHTER, EIGHTEEN,
> FORTY-SIX, OPEN, PARENT, THREE, ZERO, ZIP

```
B   X   D   A   U   G   H   T   E   R
A   Y   I   P   K   6   I   L   I   I
C   P   E   A   V   E   R   A   G   E
K   T   D   L   B   D   W   L   H   R
P   A   R   E   N   T   O   D   T   F
A   H   V   B   N   T   H   R   E   E
C   W   Z   I   P   I   I   Q   E   S
K   D   E   W   M   O   P   E   N   L
P   C   R   X   W   O   D   A   U   O
U   F   O   R   T   Y   -   S   I   X
```

 Community Challenge

Work with a partner. Where do you get a driver's license?

_____

Place

_____

Address   Telephone

Welcome to our house

Where is everyone?

A Listen.

1. kitchen

2. living room

3. bedroom

4. dining room

5. bathroom

6. yard

Listen and say.

 B Listen.

Will: Where is Justin?

Sandy: He's in the dining room.

Will: Where is Arthur?

Sandy: He's in the yard.

Listen and say.

 C Talk with a partner. Look at page 42.

A: Where is _____?

B: He's | in the _____.
       She's |

WORD LIST

Andy/bathroom
Justin/dining room
Ann/yard

A Listen.

1. table

2. sofa

3. bed

4. lamp

5. CD player

6. fireplace

7. dresser

8. rug

Listen and say.

B Listen.

Carlos:	Is there a fireplace in the living room?
Man:	Yes, there is.
Carlos:	Is there a lamp in the bedroom?
Man:	No, there isn't.

Listen and say.

C Talk with a partner.

A: Is there a _____ in the _____?

B: │ Yes, there is.
     │ No, there isn't.

WORD LIST

lamp/living room
bed/bedroom
sofa/bedroom
dresser/bedroom

A **Listen.**

1. shower   **2.** hall   **3.** sink   **4.** stove   **5.** window

6. microwave oven   **7.** closet   **8.** refrigerator   **9.** tub   **10.** barbecue

Listen and say.

 B **Listen and circle.**

'There's a window.' But 'There **are** two windows.'

1. (tub)	shower	**4.** closet	window
2. stove	barbecue	**5.** hall	window
3. sink	microwave oven	**6.** table	refrigerator

C **Complete.**

yard	~~kitchen~~	bathroom	living room

1. There's a sink in the ____kitchen____.

2. There's a shower in the _____.

3. There's a barbecue in the _____.

4. There are two windows in the _____.

(A) Listen.

1. I live in **a house**.   **2.** I live in **a rented room**.   **3.** I live in **an apartment**.

Listen and say.

(B) Talk with classmates.

A: Where do you live?

B: I live in (a/an) _____.

(C) Write. Work with a partner.

an apartment	a rented room	a house

1. _____a house_____   **2.** _____   **3.** _____

4. _____   **5.** _____   **6.** _____

A Listen and read.

Carlos's new apartment   Paul's garage

Carlos is happy with his new apartment. There is a bed and a dresser.
There are five chairs. But Carlos needs a table. He needs other furniture,
too. Paul has furniture for Carlos. The furniture is in his garage.

  ## B Listen.

Paul: What do you need?

Carlos: I need a table.

Paul: Do you need a refrigerator?

Carlos: No, I don't. Thanks.

Listen and say.

 ## C Talk with a partner.

A: What do you need?

B: I need a _____.

A: Do you need a _____?

B: No, I don't. Thanks.

WORD LIST

bed
desk
dresser
refrigerator

A Listen and circle.

1.

2.

3.

4.

B ✓ Check.

Where do you ____?	living room	kitchen	bathroom	bedroom
1. study	✓			✓
2. cook				
3. shower				
4. sleep				
5. eat				

A **Listen.**

1.

in the city

2.

in the country

3.

at the beach

4.

in the suburbs

Listen and say.

  B **Listen and read.**

Leo's dream house

My dream house is in the city. There is a kitchen, a dining room, and a living room. My dream house also has five bedrooms for my family. There are three bathrooms. I love my dream house.

 C **Write. Complete the sentences.**

1. My dream house is _____.

2. There is _____.

3. My dream house also has _____.

4. There are _____.

5. I love my dream house.

D **Read your sentences to your classmates.**

A **Listen.**

1. 12 20   5. 16 60

2. 13 30   6. 17 70

3. 14 40   7. 18 80

4. 15 50   8. 19 90

Listen and say.

  B **Listen and circle.**

1. 60 (16)   5. 30 13

2. 90 19   6. 17 70

3. 40 14   7. 20 12

4. 18 80   8. 15 50

 C **Listen and write.**

1. My address is _____ 50 _____ Beach Street.

2. The house is _____ years old.

3. The rented room is at _____ Hall Road.

4. There are _____ apartments.

5. There are _____ windows.

6. I have _____ tables.

7. We need _____ chairs in the dining room.

8. He has _____ pens.

9. The house has _____ rooms.

10. There are _____ lamps in the garage.

A Listen and read.

Garage Sales

Americans love garage sales. There are books and furniture for sale. The books and furniture are good. But they are not new. Garage sales are fun.

  B Listen and match.

Sandy's students are at a garage sale. What do they need?

1. _b_ Isabel   **a.** bike
2. ___ Carlos   ~~**b.**~~ lamp
3. ___ Don   **c.** CDs
4. ___ Maria   **d.** backpack

  C Listen.

Seller: What do you need?

Maria: I need a bike.

Seller: Good! I have a bike for sale.

Listen and say.

 D Talk with a partner.

A: What do you need?

B: I need a _____.

A: Good! I have a _____ for sale.

WORD LIST

backpack
bike
CD
fan
pan
toaster

10 Review

A Listen and circle.

1. There is a sink in the _____.   kitchen   (bathroom)
2. There are books in the _____.   bedroom   garage
3. Paul lives in the _____.   city   suburbs
4. Tomiko is _____.   13   30

B Listen and ✓ check.

1. ✓ In the dining room.   ___ An apartment.

2. ___ A table.   ___ Yes, there is.

3. ___ I need a pen.   ___ No, I don't. Thanks.

4. ___ Yes, I do. Thanks.   ___ In the yard.

C Complete the chart. Work with classmates.

Room	Furniture and Things in the Room
1. bathroom	shower, tub, _____
2. living room	
3. kitchen	

Complete.

chairs	~~kitchen~~	stove	table

This is Maria's ___kitchen___.
It has a refrigerator, a sink, and a
_____.
There are four _____, too.
Maria needs a _____.

Learning Log

Write five words you remember.

Verbs	Furniture	Rooms
eat	chair	bedroom

✓ **Check what you can do.**

1. I can name rooms and furniture.	____
2. I can say what I have and what I need.	____
3. I can write about my dream house.	____
4. I can say and understand numbers.	____
5. I can _____.	____

Looking Back

What do you see on page 42? Write three more words in your Learning Log.

I play soccer on Saturday.

Where are the people?

A Listen.

Leo: I read the newspaper.

Paul: I work on my computer.

Justin: I brush my teeth.

Andy: I play basketball.

Carlos: I watch TV.

Maria: I eat breakfast.

Sandy: I talk on the phone.

Listen and say.

B Listen and circle.

1.

2.

3.

4.

C Listen.

Sandy: What do you do every day?

Leo: I read the newspaper.

Listen and say.

D Talk with a partner.

A: What do you do every day?

B: I _____.

WORD LIST

brush my teeth
eat breakfast
play basketball
read the newspaper

A **Listen.**

Sunday	Monday	Tuesday	Wednesday	Thursday	Friday	Saturday
	1	2	3	4	5	6
7	8	9	10	11	12	13

Listen and say.

 B **Listen and circle.**

1. My sisters study on _____.   (Monday)   Tuesday
2. My brothers cook dinner on _____.   Tuesday   Thursday
3. I go to garage sales on _____.   Saturday   Sunday
4. Paul and Leo play basketball on _____.   Saturday   Sunday

 C **Listen and write.**

1. I play soccer on ____Thursday____.

2. We go to my mother's house on _____.

3. My nieces go to garage sales on _____.

4. I go to class on _____.

5. I cook dinner on _____.

6. Grace and I study on _____.

A **Listen.**

January	February	March	April	May	June
July	August	September	October	November	December

Listen and say.

 B **Listen.**

Don: When is your birthday?

Isabel: It's in October.

Listen and say.

 C **Talk with three classmates.**

A: When is your birthday?

B: It's in _____.

 D **Write.**

Apr.	Aug.	Dec.	Feb.	~~Jan.~~	Jul.
Jun.	May	Mar.	Nov.	Oct.	Sept.

1. January = ___Jan.___
2. February = _____
3. March = _____
4. April = _____
5. May = _____
6. June = _____

7. July = _____
8. August = _____
9. September = _____
10. October = _____
11. November = _____
12. December = _____

Listen.

1. 10:00

2. 7:15

3. 1:45

4. 3:30

5. 2:00

6. 4:45

7. 12:30

8. 8:15

For: 10:00
Say: It's
ten o'clock.

Listen and say.

 Listen.

Don: What time is it?
Leo: It's 10:00.

Listen and say.

 Talk with a partner. Look at the clocks.

A: What time is it?

B: It's _____.

A **Listen.**

1. 6:00

2. 8:15

3. 3:30

4. 5:45

Listen and say.

  B **Listen and circle.**

1.	6:30	(7:30)	**4.**	2:00	2:15
2.	8:30	8:45	**5.**	4:00	5:00
3.	12:15	12:45	**6.**	9:15	9:45

C **Complete. Read your sentences to classmates.**

1. I get up at _____6:00_____.

2. I go to school/work at _____.

3. I eat lunch at _____.

4. I go home at _____.

5. I go to bed at _____.

A Listen.

Grace: I'd like to make an appointment for a haircut.

Woman: Can you come on Friday at 11:45?

Grace: Friday at 11:45? That's fine.

Listen and say.

B Talk with a partner.

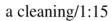

a cleaning/1:15   a tune-up/3:30   a haircut/11:45

A: I'd like to make an appointment for _____.

B: Can you come on Friday at _____?

A: Friday at _____? That's fine.

C Listen and write the times.

NOVEMBER						
Sunday	**Monday**	**Tuesday**	**Wednesday**	**Thursday**	**Friday**	**Saturday**
12	**13** haircut 5:30	**14**	**15** tune-up _____	**16**	**17** cleaning _____	**18**

60

A Listen and read.

NOVEMBER						
Sunday	Monday	Tuesday	Wednesday	Thursday	Friday	Saturday
			1 study	2 study	3 study	4 study
5 study	6 study	7 study	8 study	9 study	10 study	11 study
12 study	13 study	14 study	15 study	16 study	17 study	18 study
19	20	21	22	23	24	25

1. I study English every day.

NOVEMBER						
Sunday	Monday	Tuesday	Wednesday	Thursday	Friday	Saturday
			1 shop for food	2	3	4
5	6	7	8 shop for food	9	10	11
12	13	14	15 shop for food	16	17	18
19	20	21	22	23	24	25

2. I shop for food once a week.

NOVEMBER						
Sunday	Monday	Tuesday	Wednesday	Thursday	Friday	Saturday
			1	2	3	4
5	6	7	8	9	10	11
12	13	14	15	16	17	18 get a haircut
19	20	21	22	23	24	25

3. I get a haircut once a month.

B Listen.

Sandy: How often do you cook dinner?

Leo: Every day.

Tien: Once a week.

Carlos: Once a month.

Listen and say.

C Talk with a partner.

A: How often do you _____?

B: | Every day.
Once a week.
Once a month.

WORD LIST

cook breakfast
get a haircut
study English
talk on the phone

61

A Listen.

1ˢᵗ first	2ⁿᵈ second	3ʳᵈ third	4ᵗʰ fourth	5ᵗʰ fifth	6ᵗʰ sixth	7ᵗʰ seventh
8ᵗʰ eighth	9ᵗʰ ninth	10ᵗʰ tenth	11ᵗʰ eleventh	12ᵗʰ twelfth	13ᵗʰ thirteenth	14ᵗʰ fouteenth

Listen and say.

B Write the number.

1. __14ᵗʰ__ fourteen   3. _____ twelfth   5. _____ tenth

2. _____ third   4. _____ first   6. _____ second

C Listen and circle.

1. (5ᵗʰ)   15ᵗʰ   4. 4ᵗʰ   14ᵗʰ

2. 3ʳᵈ   13ᵗʰ   5. 3ʳᵈ   13ᵗʰ

3. 2ⁿᵈ   12ᵗʰ   6. 1ˢᵗ   11ᵗʰ

D Listen.

Woman: What is your date of birth?

Grace: March 16, 1964.

Listen and say.

For: 2005

Say: two

thousand five

E Ask three classmates.

A: What is your date of birth?

B: _____.

(A) Read.

Medical History

Lee	Grace	--	3/16/64
Last Name	First Name	MI	Date of Birth

(B) Complete the form.

Hilltop Health

Medical History

3/16/64 =
March 16, 1964

Last Name	First Name	MI	Date of Birth

(C) Write information about your class and appointments for this week.

Month: _____

Sunday	Monday	Tuesday	Wednesday	Thursday	Friday	Saturday
	10:00 class					

A Listen and write.

1. My birthday is _____October_____ 12.

2. Paul's birthday is _____ 4.

3. My class is at _____.

4. I study on _____.

B Listen and ✓ check the answer.

1. ✓ Once a week.   ___ Saturday.
2. ___ Saturday.   ___ March 16, 1964.
3. ___ December.   ___ I read the newspaper.
4. ___ 3:00.   ___ October 31.
5. ___ Sunday at 5:00?   ___ Saturday at 5:00?
6. ___ It's in February.   ___ February 18, 1991.

C Listen and circle.

1. (7:00)   7th   4. 22   2:30
2. 6th   6:30   5. 13th   30th
3. 10th   11th   6. 9:45   5:45

D **Listen and write.**

6:00	8:00 a.m.	April	~~Monday~~

Cleaning Appointment	**Jane's Haircuts**
On: _____Monday_____ ,	**Hours**
_____ 21,	**Tuesday to Saturday**
at _____	9:30 a.m. to _____ p.m.
Edward J. Weiss, D.D.S.	310 Cook Road, Middletown, MI
517 Old Road,	
Santa Cruz, CA	

E **Learning Log**

Write five words you remember.

Days	**Months**	**Ordinal Numbers**
Sunday	June	fifth

 Check what you can do.

1. I can ask for and say the time.	_____
2. I can name the days of the week and the months of the year.	_____
3. I can make appointments.	_____
4. I can say and write ordinal numbers from 1-14.	_____
5. I can _____.	_____

Looking Back

Look at page 54. What do you do every day?
Write three more words in your Learning Log.

Unit 6 Let's go shopping.

Men's Clothing

Men's Shoes

SALE

REST ROOMS

Women's SHOES

JEWELRY

Women's Clothing

REST ROOMS

Where are the students?

What do you see?

A Listen.

1. a shirt   **2.** a coat   **3.** a sweater   **4.** shoes

5. a watch   **6.** a dress   **7.** pants   **8.** a suit

Listen and say.

B Listen.

Maria: Excuse me. I'm looking for a coat.

Clerk: Follow me, please.

Maria: Thank you.

Listen and say.

C Talk with a partner.

A: Excuse me. I'm looking for _____.

B: Follow me, please.

A: Thank you.

> **WORD LIST**
>
> a coat
> a dress
> pants
> shoes

D Match.

1. _d_   **a.** a coat

2. __   **b.** a watch

3. __   **c.** pants

4. __   ~~**d.**~~ shoes

67

(A) Listen.

1. a blouse

2. a bathing suit

3. a skirt

4. a jacket

5. sneakers

Listen and say.

(B) Listen.

Clerk: May I help you?

Carlos: Yes, I'm looking for a bathing suit.

Listen and say.

(C) Talk with a partner.

A: May I help you?

B: Yes, I'm looking for _____ .

WORD LIST

a bathing suit
a blouse
sneakers

(D) Complete.

1. Isabel is looking for a _____ .

2. Grace is looking for _____ .

A Listen.

white   black   brown   pink   red   yellow   green   blue   purple

Listen and say.

 B Listen and circle.

1.   2.

3.   4.

5.   6.

 C Listen.

Sandy: What color is your jacket?

Grace: Purple.

Sandy: What color are your sneakers?

Grace: Yellow.

Listen and say.

D Talk with a partner about clothes.

A: What color is your _____?

B: _____.
    (color)

A: What color are your _____?

B: _____.
    (color)

WORD LIST

dress
pants
shirt
shoes

Grace: What are you wearing to the party?

Maria: I'm wearing a blue dress. What is Carlos wearing?

Grace: He's wearing a brown suit.

Listen and say.

B **Talk with a partner.**

A: What are you wearing?

B: I'm wearing a ⸺⸺⸺ ⸺⸺⸺.
        (color)   (clothing)

C **Talk with a partner. Look at the picture on page 66.**

A: What is ⸺⸺⸺ wearing?

B: He's ⎫ wearing (a) ⸺⸺⸺ ⸺⸺⸺.
        She's ⎭   (color)   (clothing)

WORD LIST

blue	dress
brown	jacket
green	shirt
yellow	skirt

A **Listen.**

Isabel: What's your favorite color?

Tien: Red. And you?

Isabel: Blue.

Listen and say.

B **Talk with a partner.**

A: What's your favorite color?

B: _____. And you?

A: _____.

C **Ask classmates.**

You: What's your favorite color?

Arturo: Brown.

You: Please sign here.

brown	white	blue
name: _Arturo_	name: _____	name: _____
yellow	**black**	**red**
name: _____	name: _____	name: _____
purple	**pink**	**green**
name: _____	name: _____	name: _____

A Listen.

1. small   **2.** medium   **3.** large

Listen and say.

B ✓ **Check.**

			small	**medium**	**large**
				✓	

 C Listen and circle.

1.   small   medium   (large)   **3.**   small   medium   large

2.   small   medium   large   **4.**   small   medium   large

 D Listen.

Clerk: What size are you?

Leo: I'm a large.

Listen and say.

E Talk with a partner.

A: What size are you?

B: I'm a _____.

A Listen.

1. too short

2. too long

3. too small

4. too big

Listen and say.

B Look at Activity A. Match.

1. <u>b</u> The pants   **a.** is too small.
2. ___ The sweater   ~~**b.**~~ are too short.
3. ___ The jacket   **c.** is too big.
4. ___ The blouse   **d.** is too long.

C Write two sentences about Leo's clothes.

1.

2.

73

A Listen.

1. a penny   **2.** a nickel   **3.** a dime   **4.** a quarter

1 cent (1¢)   5 cents (5¢)   10 cents (10¢)   25 cents (25¢)

Listen and say.

B Listen.

1. 1 dollar   **2.** 5 dollars   **3.** 10 dollars   **4.** 20 dollars

$1.00 $5.00 $10.00 $20.00

Listen and say.

C Match.

1. ___   **a.** $13.85

2. ___      **b.** $47.47

3. ___       **c.** $10.10

74

Read.

Isabel is buying a sweater at Spring Department Store. The sweater is $26.25.
She is writing a check.

Isabel Lopez
102 E 21st Street
Lakeland, CA 95555

1179

DATE Nov. 19, 200_   2-5654-1234

PAY
TO THE
ORDER OF _Spring Department Store_ $ | 26.25 |

Twenty-six and 25/100 ~~~~~~~~~ **DOLLARS**

Lakeland
City Bank

MEMO ___sweater___   _Isabel Lopez_

⑂012345⑂ ⑊123456543⑊01234567⑂

Write a check.

You are buying sneakers at Spring Department Store. The sneakers are
$47.25. Write a check.

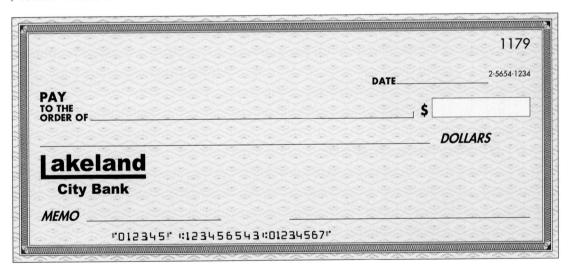

1179

DATE_____ 2-5654-1234

PAY
TO THE
ORDER OF _____ $ |_____|

_____ **DOLLARS**

Lakeland
City Bank

MEMO _____ _____

⑂012345⑂ ⑊123456543⑊01234567⑂

A Match.

_____   _____   _____   __1__

1. She's wearing a purple suit with a white blouse, and black shoes.

2. He's wearing blue pants, a green shirt, and white sneakers.

3. She's wearing a brown dress and brown shoes.

4. He's wearing brown pants, brown sneakers, and a yellow T-shirt.

B Listen and ✓ check.

1. ___ They are too small.   ✓ I'm a medium.

2. ___ Yes, I'm looking for a dress.   ___ I'm wearing the dress.

3. ___ It's purple.   ___ He's wearing a brown suit.

4. ___ Yellow.   ___ Two dollars.

C Play *Guess Who!*

Leo: She's wearing a white shirt and green pants. Guess who!

Sandy: Is it Isabel?

Leo: No. Guess again.

Sandy: Is it Maria?

Leo: Yes! Your turn.

Think about a classmate. Play *Guess Who!*

You: He's | wearing (a) _____.
      She's |

D **What are you wearing today?**

1. I'm wearing _____

2. _____

3. _____

E **Learning Log**

Write five words you remember.

Colors	Clothing	Money
purple	a dress	a penny

✓ **Check what you can do.**

1. I can ask for help in a store.	___
2. I can name colors and sizes.	___
3. I can say what I'm wearing.	___
4. I can write a check.	___
5. I can _____.	___

Looking Back

Look at page 66. Write three more words in your Learning Log.

Grammar Spotlight
for Units 4-6

A Singular and Plural Nouns

	Singular	Plural
Most nouns	a coat a room	two coats four rooms
Nouns that end in -<u>ch</u>, -<u>sh</u>, -<u>s</u>, or -<u>x</u>	a wat<u>ch</u> a dres<u>s</u>	12 wat<u>ch</u>es 200 dres<u>s</u>es

Circle the plural nouns.

Isabel lives in a rented room. She has a closet, a dresser and two (chairs.)
Her books are on the desk. Her dresses and coats are in the closet. There are
two watches on the dresser.

Isabel's mother, father, and sister live in a house. Their house has seven
rooms. It has a kitchen, a dining room, a living room, four bedrooms, and two
bathrooms.

B A/an

Paul lives in **a house**.	Use **a** for **one** noun.
Maria lives in **an apartment**.	Use **an** before **a, e, i, o**, or **u**.

Write *a* or *an*.

I live in ___a___ rented room. I'm looking for ____ apartment.

I'm looking for ____ kitchen, a living room, two bedrooms, and ____ bathroom.

I'm looking for ____ apartment building with ____ elevator.

78

Simple Present Tense

I	**read** books.
You	**speak** English.
We	**eat** breakfast.
They	**work** every day.

He	**reads** books.
She	**speaks** English.
It	**eats** breakfast.

Write.

1. (read)   I ___read___ the newspaper every day.

2. (work)   Maria _____ on a computer once a week.

3. (play)   Justin and Andy _____ soccer on Saturday.

4. (eat)   Paul _____ breakfast every day.

5. (cook)   We _____ on Thursday.

6. (talk)   Sandy _____ on the phone every day.

7. (need)   Tien and Grace _____ books.

8. (sleep)   They _____ in the bedroom.

9. (speak)   I _____ Spanish.

10. (live)   He _____ at 11 Green Street.

**Match.**

1. _c_ Where do you live?   **a.** She's wearing a red dress.

2. ___ What do you need?   **b.** 10:45.

3. ___ Where's the refrigerator?   **c.** In an apartment.

4. ___ What's she wearing?   **d.** It's in the kitchen.

5. ___ When is your birthday?   **e.** I need a desk.

6. ___ What time is it?   **f.** It's in June.

B **What does Carlos need?**

Talk with a partner. Draw the furniture Carlos needs.

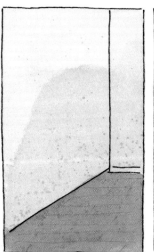

C **Write three sentences about Carlos's new furniture on page 80.**

There is a sofa in the living room.

1. _____

2. _____

3. _____

D **Community Challenge**

Read.

Maria is buying a sweater and shirts on the Internet. This is the check-out page.

IS *Internet Shopping.com*

Ship To: Maria Cruz
115 Brown Road
Los Angeles, CA 90037

Item	How many?	Size	Color	Price	Subtotal
sweater	1	small	black	$28.95	$28.95
shirt	3	medium	white	$11.35	$34.05

Subtotal	$63.00
Shipping & Handling	$4.95
Total:	**$67.95**

THANK YOU FOR SHOPPING WITH US!

✓ **Check *True* or *False*.**

	True	False
1. Maria is buying a sweater and three shirts.	✓	___
2. The sweater is black.	___	___
3. She needs a medium sweater.	___	___
4. The shirts are large.	___	___
5. Maria lives in Los Angeles.	___	___

I'm so hungry!

ICE CREAM

DAIRY

MEAT

PRODUCE

BAKERY

SHOPPING LIST

ICE CREAM

ICE CREAM

ICE CREAM

EGGS

What food do you see?

A **Listen.**

1. eggs   **2.** ice cream   **3.** carrots

4. apples   **5.** potatoes   **6.** milk

Listen and say.

  B **Listen.**

Carlos: We need eggs.

Antonio: That's right. We need apples, too.

Listen and say.

 C **Talk with a partner.**

A: We need _____.

B: That's right. We need _____, too.

WORD LIST

apples
carrots
eggs
ice cream
milk
potatoes

83

A Listen.

1. cake   **2.** bread   **3.** beef   **4.** chicken

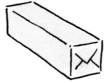

5. oranges   **6.** butter   **7.** cheese

Listen and say.

B Listen.

Grace: Do we need butter?

Ben: Yes, we do.

Grace: Do we need oranges?

Ben: No, we don't.

Listen and say.

C Talk with a partner.

A: Do we need _____?

B: | Yes, we do.
     | No, we don't.

WORD LIST

beef
bread
cheese
chicken
oranges

A **Listen.**

| Aisle 1 Fruits and Vegetables | Aisle 2 Meat | Aisle 3 Bakery | Aisle 4 Dairy |

Grace: Excuse me. I'm looking for apples.

Clerk: Let's see. Aisle 1.

Listen and say.

  B **Listen and complete the chart.**

	Food	Aisle 1 Fruits and Vegetables	Aisle 2 Meat	Aisle 3 Bakery	Aisle 4 Dairy
1.	apples	✓			
2.	beef				
3.	chicken				
4.	cheese				
5.	cake				
6.	oranges				
7.	milk				

C **Talk with a partner. Use the chart.**

A: Excuse me. I'm looking for _____.
(food)

B: Let's see. Aisle _____.

A Listen.

1. breakfast **2.** lunch **3.** dinner

Listen and say.

B Listen.

Sunday	Monday	Tuesday	Wednesday	Thursday	Friday	Saturday
bread and cheese	bread and cheese	bread and cheese	bread and cheese	bread and cheese	eggs	bread and cheese

Leo: What do you have for breakfast?

Sandy: I usually have bread and cheese. Sometimes I have eggs.

Listen and say.

C Talk with a partner.

A: What do you have for breakfast?

B: I usually have _____. Sometimes I have _____.

86

A Listen.

Don: It's 12:30. I'm so hungry!

Paul: Me, too. Let's have lunch.

Listen and say.

B Talk with a partner.

A: It's _____. I'm so hungry!

B: Me, too. Let's have _____.

WORD LIST

8:00/breakfast
1:30/lunch
6:30/dinner

C Complete.

I usually have breakfast at ____6:00____. Then I have lunch at

____12 ᵒᵖ____. I go home and have dinner at ____6:00____. I usually

have _____ for dinner.
        (food)

A Listen.

LUNCH SPECIALS
$4.25
INCLUDING A DRINK
AND DESSERT

PIZZA   TUNA SANDWICH   HAMBURGER   CHERRY PIE   COFFEE   TEA   SODA

Listen and say.

B Listen.

Server:	May I help you?
Paul:	Yes. I'll have a tuna sandwich, please.
Server:	Anything else?
Paul:	Yes. I'll have a coffee, too.

Listen and say.

C Talk with a partner.

A: May I help you?

B: Yes. I'll have a _____, please.

A: Anything else?

B: Yes. I'll have a _____, too.

WORD LIST

coffee
pizza
soda
tea
tuna sandwich

Listen.

Leo: Do you have eggs for lunch?

Grace: Yes, I do.

Paul: No, I don't.

Listen and say.

B **Talk with four classmates.**

A: Do you have _____

for _____?

B: | Yes, I do.
Sometimes.
No, I don't.

WORD LIST

coffee/breakfast
milk/dinner
beef/lunch
eggs/dinner
apples/breakfast
a tuna sandwich/lunch

C **Write three questions.**

1. Do you have _____ for breakfast?

2. Do you _____ _____ for lunch?

3. Do you _____ _____ for dinner?

Ask a classmate your questions.

D **Write.**

1. I have _____ for breakfast.

2. I sometimes have _____ for lunch.

3. I sometimes have _____ for dinner.

A Listen.

1. a bottle   2. a can   3. a bag   4. a package   5. a box   6. a bunch   7. a jar

Listen and say.

B Listen and circle.

1. (a bunch)   a box   4. (a package)   a bunch
2. (a bag)   a jar   5. a bag   (a box)
3. a bottle   (a can)   6. (a bottle)   a can

C Play *What Do We Need?*

We need coffee.

We need coffee and bananas.

We need coffee, bananas, and . . .

  A **Listen and read.**

A Potluck Dinner

Once a month Sandy's class has a potluck dinner. The students bring different foods. They bring fruits, vegetables, meat, drinks, or desserts. Sandy's students make special foods from their countries. The potluck dinners are fun, and the food is interesting.

B ✓ **Check *True* or *False*.**

		True	False
1.	Sandy's class has a potluck dinner once a week. *month*		✓
2.	~~Sandy~~ *students* brings the food to the potluck dinners.		✓
3.	Some students bring desserts.	✓	
4.	The students bring foods from their countries.	✓	
5.	The potluck lunches are fun.		✓

C **Write.**

Your class has a potluck dinner. What food do you bring?

Food: _____

10 Review

A **Listen and ✓ check the food Maria needs to buy.**

1.	☑ chicken	☐	bread
2.	☐ hamburger	☐	milk
3.	☐ apples	☐	juice
4.	☐ oranges	☐	eggs
5.	☐ beef	☐	cheese

B **Listen and circle the answer.**

1. **a.** Let's have lunch. **b.** Let's see. Aisle 2.
2. **a.** Cereal, juice, and fruit. **b.** In the dairy section.
3. **a.** Good. **b.** Oranges are in Aisle 5.
4. **a.** I'll have the dinner special. **b.** A bottle of oil.
5. **a.** I usually have cereal. **b.** Yes, I'll have a hamburger.
6. **a.** Yes, I'll have a coffee. **b.** Sometimes I have soup.

C **Ask three classmates.**

You: What is your favorite food?

NAME:	Carlos			
FAVORITE FOOD:	ice cream			

D Tell a partner what food you need.

You: I need sugar.

E Write.

1. My favorite breakfast is _____.
2. My favorite lunch is _____.

F Learning Log

Write five words you remember.

Food	Meals	Containers
apples	lunch	a bag

 Check what you can do.

1. I can name foods.	___
2. I can talk about containers.	___
3. I can ask for help in a supermarket.	___
4. I can order food.	___
5. I can _____.	___

Looking Back

What food do you see on page 82? Now write three more words in your Learning Log.

Unit 8 How's the weather?

Specials

Where is Tien?

Where is Carlos?

94

A **Listen.**

1. It's sunny.

2. It's snowy.

3. It's hot.

4. It's cold.

5. It's windy.

6. It's rainy.

Listen and say.

 B **Listen.**

Tien: How's the weather?

Carlos: It's sunny.

Listen and say.

C **Talk with a partner about the pictures in Activity A.**

A: How's the weather?

B: It's _____ .

A **Listen and circle.**

1.     2.

3.     4.

B **Match.**

1. <u>d</u>   **a.** It's windy.

2. ___   **b.** It's snowy.

3. ___   **c.** It's hot.

4. ___   ~~**d.**~~ It's cold.

5. ___   **e.** It's rainy.

6. ___   **f.** It's sunny.

96

A Listen.

1. winter   **2.** spring   **3.** summer   **4.** fall

Listen and say.

B Complete.

1. It's _____.

2. It's _____.

C Listen.

Grace: What's your favorite season?

Leo: Winter.

Listen and say.

D Talk with a partner.

A: What's your favorite season?

B: _____.

WORD LIST

winter
spring
summer
fall

97

A **Listen.**

1. walking   **2.** playing soccer   **3.** dancing   **4.** reading

5. swimming   **6.** listening to music   **7.** cooking   **8.** watching TV

Listen and say.

 B **Listen.**

Will:	What are you doing?
Sandy:	I'm working. What about you?
Will:	I'm cooking.

Listen and say.

C **Talk with a partner.**

A: What are you doing?

B: I'm ＿＿＿＿＿＿＿. What about you?

A: I'm ＿＿＿＿＿＿＿.

> **WORD LIST**
>
> playing soccer/watching TV
> swimming/reading
> dancing/listening to music

A Listen and circle.

1.

2.

3.

4.

B Listen.

Sandy: What's Justin doing?

Will: He's playing basketball.

Listen and say.

C Talk with a partner.

A: What's _____ doing?

B: He's ⎰ _____.
      She's ⎱

WORD LIST

Grace/swimming
Leo/dancing
Ben/walking
Maria/talking

A **Listen.**

Isabel: What do you like doing in the spring?

Grace: I like playing soccer.

Isabel: What about in the winter?

Grace: I like listening to music.

Listen and say.

B **Talk with a partner.**

A: What do you like doing in the _____?
(season)

B: I like _____.
(activity)

A: What about in the _____?
(season)

B: I like _____.
(activity)

C **Ask four classmates.**

You: What do you do like doing in the _____?

Name	Season	Activity
Grace	spring	playing soccer
1.	summer	
2.	fall	
3.	winter	
4.	spring	

A **Listen and read.**

1. It's summer. It's hot and cloudy.

2. It's fall. It's sunny and cool.

3. It's winter. It's rainy and windy.

 B **Write.**

1. In winter, it's _____ and _____.

2. In fall, it's _____ and _____.

3. In summer, it's _____ and _____.

101

A **Listen and write the numbers.**

1. It's very hot.

   It's _____105_____ ° F.

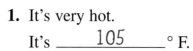

F =
Fahrenheit
C =
Celsius

2. It's hot.

   It's _____ ° F.

3. It's cool.

   It's _____ ° F.

4. It's cold.

   It's _____ ° F.

A Read the weather map.

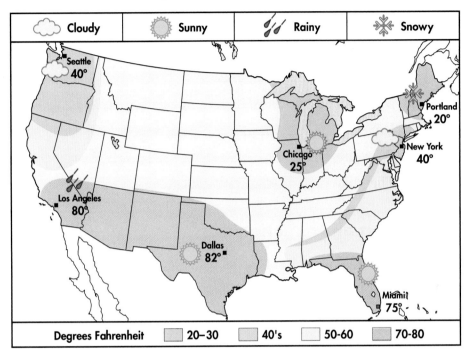

| Cloudy | Sunny | Rainy | Snowy |

Seattle 40°
Portland 20°
New York 40°
Chicago 25°
Los Angeles 80°
Dallas 82°
Miami 75°

Degrees Fahrenheit: 20–30 | 40's | 50-60 | 70-80

B Complete the chart.

City	Temperature	Sunny	Rainy	Snowy	Cloudy
Seattle	40° F				✓
Los Angeles					
Dallas					
Portland					
New York					

C Write a weather report for your city today.

This is a weather report for Chicago.
The temperature is 25°F. The weather is sunny and cold.

_____

_____

10 Review

A **Listen and write.**

1. How's the _____weather_____ ?

2. It's _____ .

3. My favorite season is _____ .

4. I'm _____ soccer.

5. What are you _____ ?

6. They like _____ .

B **Listen and ✓ check.**

1. ___ Yes, it is.   ✓ It's hot and sunny.

2. ___ It's snowy.   ___ Winter.

3. ___ Summer.   ___ It's hot!

4. ___ It's snowy.   ___ I'm playing soccer.

5. ___ Yes, she is.   ___ She's working.

6. ___ It's windy.   ___ I like playing basketball.

C **Listen and circle.**

1. 16°F   (60°F)

2. windy   cloudy

3. 55°F   snowy

4. 14°F   40°F

5. cold   cloudy

6. 95°F   rainy

D **Write.**

1. My favorite season is _____ .

2. The weather is _____ and _____ today.

3. The temperature is _____ today.

E **Ask three classmates.**

Leo: What do you like doing in the winter?

Tien: I like watching TV.

Leo: What about in the spring?

Tien: I like walking.

Name	Winter?	Spring?	Summer?	Fall?
Tien	watching TV	walking	swimming	reading
1.				
2.				
3.				

 F **Learning Log**

Write five words you remember.

Seasons	Weather	Activities
spring	cloudy	reading

✓ Check what you can do.

1. I can ask about the weather.	___
2. I can talk about the seasons.	___
3. I can say what I'm doing.	___
4. I can read a weather map.	___
5. I can _____.	___

Looking Back

What's the weather on page 94? Now write three more words in your Learning Log.

10

A Listen. Look at page 106.

1. police station **2.** bank **3.** drugstore **4.** hospital

5. fire station **6.** gas station **7.** library **8.** post office

Listen and say.

B Listen.

Tien: Where are you going?

Grace: I'm going to the post office.

Listen and say.

C Talk with a partner.

A: Where are you going?

B: I'm going to the _____.

WORD LIST

bank
gas station
hospital
library

D Match.

1. b   **a.** post office

2. a   **b.** drugstore

3. d   **c.** hospital

4. c   **d.** fire station

A Look at page 106. Write the places.

| fire station | hospital | drugstore | gas station |

1. _____fire station_____
2. _____drugstore_____
3. _____hospital_____
4. _____gas station_____

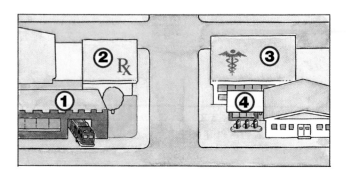

B Listen.

Woman: Excuse me. Where's the gas station?

Grace: It's on 20th Street.

Woman: Thanks.

Listen and say.

C Talk with a partner.

A: Excuse me. Where's the

_____?

B: It's on _____.

A: Thanks.

WORD LIST

gas station/20th Street
hospital/19th Street
drugstore/South Avenue

A **Listen.**

1. laundromat

2. movie theater

3. supermarket

4. bus stop

5. park

6. restaurant

Listen and say.

  B **Listen.**

Isabel: Is there a restaurant in your neighborhood?

Leo: Yes, there is.

Maria: No, there isn't.

Listen and say.

 C **Talk with a partner.**

A: Is there a _____

in your neighborhood?

B: | Yes, there is.
| No, there isn't.

WORD LIST

bus stop
laundromat
movie theater
park
supermarket

A Listen and read.

Maria is <u>in</u> the bank. The bank is <u>between</u> the drugstore and the supermarket. The drugstore is <u>next to</u> the bank.

B Listen.

Don: Where's the bank?

Paul: It's next to the drugstore.

Tien: It's between the drugstore and the supermarket.

Listen and say.

C Talk with a partner.

A: Where's the _____?

B: It's next to the _____.

WORD LIST

bank
drugstore
supermarket

A Listen and write.

1. The gas station is ___next to___ the library.
2. The hospital is ___between___ the gas station and the bank.
3. The hospital is ___on the___ 19th Street.
4. The police station is ___next to___ the hospital.
5. The post office is ___between___ the library and the hospital.
6. Don and Sumin are ___in___ the bank.
7. Leo is ___in___ the drugstore.
8. The gas station is ___on the___ South Avenue.

B Complete.

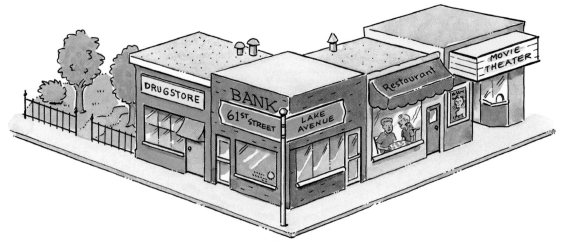

between	in	next to	~~on~~

1. The restaurant is ___on___ Lake Avenue.
2. The drugstore is ___between___ the bank and the park.
3. The movie theater is ___next to___ the restaurant.
4. Paul and Isabel are ___in___ the restaurant.

(A) Listen.

1. He's <u>near</u> the bus stop.   **2.** He's <u>far from</u> the bus stop.

Listen and say.

(B) Listen and circle.

1. (near)   far from   **4.** near   far from

2. near   far from   **5.** near   far from

3. near   far from   **6.** near   far from

(C) Listen.

Sandy: Do you live near a park?

Isabel: Yes, I do.

Paul: No, I don't.

Listen and say.

(D) Ask classmates.

You: Do you live near a park?

Isabel: Yes, I do.

You: Please sign here.

near a park?	far from a bus stop?
name: _____Isabel_____	name: _____
near a bank?	far from a supermarket?
name: _____	name: _____

112

(A) Listen.

1. see a movie   **2.** buy stamps   **3.** wash clothes   **4.** make a deposit

Listen and say.

(B) Listen.

Carlos: Where do you buy stamps?

Grace: At a post office.

Listen and say.

(C) Talk with a partner.

A: Where do you _____?

B: At a _____.

> ### WORD LIST
>
> see a movie/movie theater
> buy stamps/post office
> wash clothes/laundromat
> make a deposit/bank

(D) Write.

Where do you _____?	Place
see a movie	
wash clothes	
make a deposit	

A Listen and read.

Tien is putting money in the bank. She is depositing money into her savings account. This is her deposit slip. She is depositing a check. She is also depositing cash.

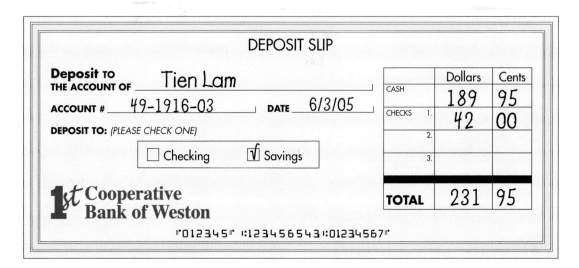

DEPOSIT SLIP

Deposit TO THE ACCOUNT OF _Tien Lam_

ACCOUNT # _49-1916-03_   **DATE** _6/3/05_

DEPOSIT TO: *(PLEASE CHECK ONE)*

☐ Checking   ☑ Savings

1st Cooperative Bank of Weston

⑊012345⑊ ⑊123456543⑊01234567⑊

	Dollars	Cents
CASH	189	95
CHECKS 1.	42	00
2.		
3.		
TOTAL	231	95

B Write the numbers.

1. The date is _June 3, 2005_.
2. Tien's account number is _49-1916-03_.
3. She is depositing $_231-95_.
4. The check is for $_42 00_.

C Complete.

1. The money goes to her ___savings___ account. (checking, ~~savings~~)
2. She's depositing _____. (one check, two checks)
3. Her cash deposit is _____. (($189.95), $231.95))
4. She is depositing a total of _____. ($123.95, $231.95)
5. June is the _____ month of the year. (fifth, sixth)

114

Using an ATM

A Listen and read.

Don is taking money from his checking account. He's making a withdrawal.

1

Insert your ATM card.

2

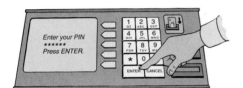
Enter your PIN
******
Press ENTER.

ATM =
Automated
Teller
Machine

3

Pick one: Withdrawal
Deposit
Balance

4

Pick one: Savings
Checking
Credit

5

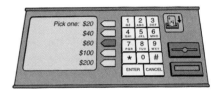
Pick one: $20
$40
$60
$100
$200

6

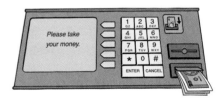
Please take
your money.

B Circle. Work with a partner.

1. Don's PIN is 2679. He presses _____. (2-6-7-9)   9-7-6-2
2. He is making a _____.   (withdrawal)   deposit
3. He is taking money from _____.   (checking)   savings
4. He is taking _____.   ($60) $200

A Listen and write.

Isabel: _____Excuse_____ me. Where is the police station?

Man: It's _____On_____ 54th Street.

Isabel: _____Thanks_____ .

  B Listen and ✓ check.

1. ✓ To the library.   ___ In the library.
2. ___ Yes, it is.   ✓ It's next to the fire station.
3. ✓ On 21st Avenue.   ___ I'm at the library.
4. ✓ No, I don't.   ___ Next to the drugstore.

 C Listen and write.

bank	movie theater	post office	~~restaurant~~

1. They're in a ___restaurant___ .   3. They're in a ___bank___ .
2. They're in a ___movie theater___ .   4. They're in a ___post office___

D **Complete the sentences about where you live.**

1. I live on _____ (Street, Avenue, Road).

2. My address is _____.

3. My house is near _____.

E **Learning Log**

Write five words or phrases you remember.

Places	Banking	Activities
post office	deposit	buying stamps

✓ **Check what you can do.**

1. I can name places in my neighborhood.	___
2. I can ask for directions.	___
3. I can read a deposit slip.	___
4. I can use an ATM.	___
5. I can _____.	___

Looking Back

Look at page 106. What new places do you know? Now write three more words in your Learning Log.

Present Continuous

I am working.	I'm working.
He is working.	He's working.
She is working.	She's working.
It is working.	It's working.
We are working.	We're working.
You are working.	You're working.
They are working.	They're working.

Write the present continuous.

1. Leo is in the park. _____He's walking_____ his dog.
He/walk

2. Ben and Grace are in a restaurant. _____ lunch.
They/eat

3. Tien is in the bank. _____ a deposit.
She/make

4. You and Don are in the library. _____ books.

5. I'm in the post office. _____ stamps.

What are you doing now? Write two sentences.

1. _I'm_____.

2. _____.

B Question Words

Question Words	Questions	Answers
Where = places	**Where's** the bread?	In Aisle 4.
	Where are Sandy and Will?	At the beach.
How = descriptions	**How's** the weather?	It's cold and rainy.
	How are your sons?	They're fine.
What = things	**What's** your favorite season?	Winter.
	What are your favorite foods?	Bread and cheese.

Match.

1. _c_ How's the weather?
2. ___ Where's the laundromat?
3. ___ What are their favorite sports?
4. ___ Where are Tien and Maria?
5. ___ What's the temperature?

a. In the bank.
b. 60°F.
c. It's hot.
d. Between the bank and the park.
e. Basketball and soccer.

Write *How, Where,* or *What.*

1. **A:** ___How___'s your brother?

   B: He's very happy.

2. **A:** _____ is he?

   B: He's in Los Angeles.

3. **A:** _____ are his favorite foods?

   B: Chicken and carrots.

4. **A:** _____'s the weather in Los Angeles?

   B: It's sunny and hot.

5. **A:** _____'s the restaurant?

   B: On Midway Avenue.

6. **A:** _____ are your children?

   B: They're fine.

Review
for
Units
7-9

A **Match.**

1. <u>f</u> How's the weather?
2. ___ What's your favorite season?
3. ___ What do you like doing in the summer?
4. ___ Where are you going?
5. ___ Where's the bank?
6. ___ Do we need milk?

   a. No, we don't.
   b. It's on Main Street.
   c. I like swimming.
   d. Spring.
   e. I'm going to the bank.
   f. It's sunny.

B **Listen and circle the correct answer.**

1.

   a. It's windy.
   b. It's rainy.

2.

   a. They're dancing.
   b. They're playing soccer.

3.

   a. It's cloudy.
   b. It's sunny.

C Complete.

Aisle	bank	~~bunch~~	jar
laundromat	like	milk	summer

1. I need a _____bunch_____ of grapes.

2. I have one _____ of peanut butter.

3. Bread is in _____ 4.

4. I wash my clothes at the _____.

5. I usually drink _____ for breakfast.

6. I like swimming in the _____.

7. I _____ listening to music.

8. I make a withdrawal from the _____.

D Community Challenge

Work with a partner. Find addresses and phone numbers in your city or town.

Name	Address	Phone number
U.S. Post Office	West 6th Street Los Angeles, CA 90020	213-382-8136
Police Station		
Library		
Bank		

You need to see a doctor.

Where are the people?

What do you see?

A Listen.

1. an earache
~~UEP~~

2. a sore throat

3. a headache

4. a broken arm

5. a toothache

6. a stomachache

7. a backache

8. a cold

Listen and say.   *throw up*
vomit

 B Listen.

Nurse: What's the matter?

Maria: I have a headache.

Listen and say.

C Talk with a partner.

A: What's the matter?

B: I have a _____.

WORD LIST

backache
cold
headache
stomachache
toothache

(A) Listen.

1. head
2. eye
3. nose
4. stomach
5. arm

6. hand
7. finger
8. leg
9. foot

[handwritten annotations on figure: ear, shoulder, neck, chest, elbow, hip, wrist, knee, ankle; on the hand: pointer, middle, ring, pinkie, thumb]

Listen and say.

(B) Listen.

Sandy: What's the matter with Don?

Leo: His hand hurts.

Listen and say.

(C) Talk with a partner.

A: What's the matter with _____?

B: His | _____ hurts.
    Her |

WORD LIST

Isabel/foot
Carlos/arm
Leo/finger
Maria/head
Grace/stomach

A Listen.

Ana: I feel bad. My ear hurts.

Maria: You need to see a doctor.

Listen and say.

B Talk with a partner.

A: I feel bad. My _____ hurts.

B: You need to see a doctor.

WORD LIST

eye
hand
leg
stomach

C Listen.

Maria: Hello. This is Maria Cruz. My daughter is sick.

Can Dr. Brown see her today?

Man: Yes. Dr. Brown can see her at 10:00.

Maria: Today at 10:00? That's fine. Thank you.

Listen and say.

D Talk with a partner.

A: Hello. This is _____. My son is sick. Can Dr. Brown see him today?
(name)

B: Yes. Dr. Brown can see him at _____.
(time)

A: Today at _____? That's fine. Thank you.
(time)

A Listen.

  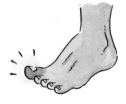 

1. a cut   **2.** a cough   **3.** an infection   **4.** a fever

Listen and say.

B Listen.

  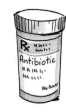 

1. a bandage   **2.** cough syrup   **3.** an antibiotic   **4.** aspirin

Listen and say.

C Listen and ✓ check.

	1. Isabel	2. Carlos	3. Don	4. Leo
a cut	✓			
a fever		✓		✓
an infection			✓	
an antibiotic			✓	
aspirin		✓		✓
a bandage	✓			

A Listen.

Don: Sumin has a cut on her arm.

Grace: That's too bad. She needs a bandage.

Listen and say.

B Talk with a partner.

A: Paul has _____.

B: That's too bad. He needs

_____.

C Listen. Complete the chart.

WORD LIST

a cough/cough syrup
a cut/a bandage
a headache/aspirin
an infection/an antibiotic

Name	What's the matter?	Body Part	Needs
1. Leo	a cut		
2. Isabel			
3. Paul			

A **Listen.**

1. exercise 2. drink water 3. get enough sleep 4. eat healthy food

Listen and say.

B ✓ **Check what you do.**

_____	I exercise.	_____	I get enough sleep.
_____	I drink water.	_____	I eat healthy food.

C **Listen.**

1. Raise your arms. 2. Touch your toes. 3. Stretch. 4. Jump.

Listen and say.

D **Listen and follow the directions. Look at your teacher.**

A Listen and read.

The Goldman Sisters

Frances and Eleanor Goldman are sisters. They are healthy. Eleanor is 81 years old. Frances is 83. They exercise and eat healthy food every day. Frances likes apples. Eleanor likes oranges. They drink water. They get enough sleep.

Eleanor likes to swim. Frances likes to walk her dog. She has a large dog. Frances says, "Be healthy. Get a dog." Eleanor says, "Be healthy. Go swimming."

B Complete.

likes apples	~~healthy~~	~~81~~	has a large dog	exercises
walks a lot	83	swims	likes oranges	

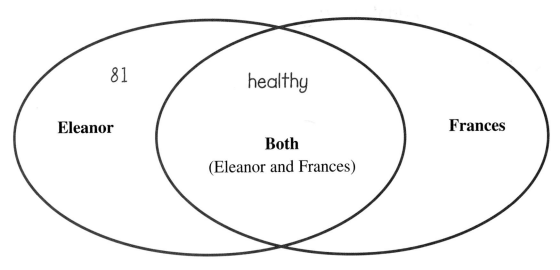

81

healthy

Eleanor

Both
(Eleanor and Frances)

Frances

C Write.

1. I _____ walk a lot _____ every day.
2. I _____ every week.
3. I _____ .
4. I _____ .

129

A **Listen.**

1. a pill **2.** a capsule **3.** a teaspoon of medicine

Listen and say.

 B **Listen.**

| 1x | 2x | 3x |

1. once **2.** twice **3.** three times

Listen and say.

C **Circle the answers in the chart.**

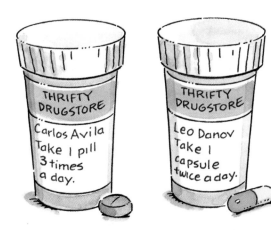

Medicine for:	It's a ___.	Take ___ a day.
1. Carlos	(pill) capsule	1 x 2 x (3x)
2. Leo	pill (capsule)	1 x (2x) 3 x

130

Health insurance

In the Community

  A **Listen and read.**

Grace has a health insurance card. She needs the card to see a doctor. Her health insurance is from her husband's work.

Community Health Care Group

Name of Insured: **Grace Lee**   ID#: **90933MC**
D.O.B.: **3/16/64**

Name of Employee: **Ben Lee**   Plan: **Family**

Grace Lee

Co-payment: **$5.00**

Co-payment=
Money you
pay to see
a doctor

 B **Fill in the form for Grace.**

WESTON
Health Center

Patient's Name: Grace Lee _____   Today's Date: _____

Date of Birth: _ _ / _ _ / _ _ _____

Name of Employee: _____

Type of Plan: (circle one) individual   family   ID#: _____

Co-payment: (circle one) YES / NO $_____

10 Review

A Write.

| a toothache   a headache |
| a sore throat   a stomachache   a cold |

1. a toothache   2. _____   3. _____

4. _____   5. _____

B Listen and ✓ check the answer.

1. ✓ I have a headache.   ___ How are you?
2. ___ Cough syrup.   ___ He feels bad.
3. ___ Yes. Dr. Wall can see you at 3:00.   ___ Her arm hurts.
4. ___ She needs an antibiotic.   ___ Her ear hurts.

C Write.

Doctor: What's the matter?

You: I have a _____ .

Doctor: That's too bad. You _____ .

Cross out the wrong word.

Health Problems	~~nose~~	a fever	an infection	a cut
Medicine	a pill	aspirin	a capsule	a backache
Body Parts	an arm	a tooth	a capsule	a knee
Be Healthy	a cold	touch your toes	stretch	walk

E **Learning Log**

Write five words you remember.

Body	Health Problems	Be Healthy
leg	a cut	walking

✓ **Check what you can do.**

1. I can talk about a health problem.	___
2. I can name body parts.	___
3. I can make an appointment.	___
4. I can take medicine.	___
5. I can _____.	___

Looking Back

What health problems are on page 122? Now write three more words in your Learning Log.

What's your job?

What jobs do you see?

A Listen. Look at page 134.

1. a custodian
2. a delivery person
3. a receptionist
4. a taxi driver

5. a cashier
6. a cook
7. a waiter
8. a gardener

Listen and say.

B Listen.

Paul: What do you do?

Tien: I'm a delivery person. And you?

Paul: I'm a custodian.

Listen and say.

C Talk with a partner.

A: What do you do?

B: I'm _____. And you?

A: I'm _____.

WORD LIST

a cashier
a cook
a delivery person
a gardener
a receptionist
a taxi driver

(A) Listen.

1. a taxi cab   **2.** pots and pans   **3.** a computer   **4.** a cash register

Listen and say.

(B) ✓ **Check who uses it.**

Jobs	A taxi cab	Pots and pans	A computer	A cash register
taxi driver	✓			
receptionist				
cook				
cashier				

 (C) Listen and circle.

1. ⟨receptionist⟩   gardener
2. cook   custodian
3. waiter   taxi driver
4. taxi driver   cashier

3 Do you like to work outdoors?

 A Listen.

1. indoors   **2.** outdoors   **3.** with people   **4.** with machines

Listen and say.

 B ✓ Check.

Jobs	Indoors	Outdoors	With People	With Machines
cashier	✓		✓	✓
gardener				
waiter				
custodian				
delivery person				

 C Listen.

Grace: Do you like to work indoors?

Don: Yes, I do. And you?

Grace: No, I don't.

Listen and say.

 D Talk with a partner.

A: Do you like to work _____?

B: | Yes, I do.
     | No, I don't.

> **WORD LIST**
> indoors
> outdoors
> with machines
> with people

A **Listen.**

1. drive   **2.** fix   **3.** use   **4.** sell

Listen and say.

B **Complete with words from Activity A.**

1. Leo can ____drive____ a car.

2. Tien can _____ things in the house.

3. Paul can _____ a computer.

4. Maria can _____ clothes in a store.

  C **Listen.**

Leo: What can you do?

Paul: I can use a computer. And you?

Leo: I can drive a car.

Listen and say.

D **Write three things you can do.**

1. I can _____.

2. I _____.

3. _____.

138

A Listen.

Man: Can you sell clothes?

Maria: Yes, I can.

Man: Can you drive a car?

Maria: No, I can't.

Listen and say.

B Talk with a partner.

A: Can you _____?

B: Yes, I can.
No, I can't.

WORD LIST

use a computer
drive a car
fix things
sell clothes
cook food

C Ask classmates.

You: Can you drive a car?

Leo: Yes, I can.

You: Please sign here.

drive a car	fix things	use machines
name: _____	name: _____	name: _____
cook food	use a computer	sell clothes
name: _____	name: _____	name: _____

A Read the want ads. Circle the jobs.

1.

Wilder Men's Shop at Low Creek Mall.
Seeking 2 cashiers.
Call Mr. Howard, the manager.
310-555-6789

2.
SAN DIEGO
TRAVEL WELL HOTEL needs a general custodian. Experienced. See Wendy the manager.

B Match.

1. _a_ Who is the manager at the Travel Well Hotel?

2. ___ What is the phone number at Wilder Men's Shop?

3. ___ Who is the manager at Wilder Men's Shop?

4. ___ Where is Wilder Men's Shop?

5. ___ Where is Travel Well Hotel?

a. Wendy

b. Mr. Howard

c. At Low Creek Mall

d. San Diego

e. 310-555-6789

C Listen and ✓ check the ad from Activity A.

Names	Ad #1	Ad #2
1. Sara	✓	
2. Ben		
3. Frank		
4. John		

140

A Listen.

Leo before
(1985)

Maria before
(1995)

Leo: I was a taxi driver in Russia. What was your job before?

Maria: I was a cashier in Mexico.

Listen and say.

B Talk with a partner.

A: I was (a/an) _____ in _____ . What was your job before?
                   (job)   (country)

B: I was (a/an) _____ in _____ .
                   (job)   (country)

C Read. Answer the questions.

Job Information

Name: Leo V. Danov

Address: 17 Apple Street, Los Angeles, CA 90001

Telephone: 2 1 3 . 5 5 5 . 8 8 9 2

Work Experience:

Job	Employer	Dates
Delivery Person	On-Time Delivery Co.	1997–2002
Taxi Driver	Swift Taxi, Inc.	1995–1996

1. What is Leo's address? _____ .
2. What is Leo's telephone number? _____ .
3. What was Leo's job from 1997-2002? _____ .
4. What was Leo's job from 1995-1996? _____ .

141

A Listen and read.

Don is a cashier. He works at Shop Rite Food Store. Don makes $10 an hour. Don works eight hours a week. He makes $80 a week.

Don has to pay taxes. He pays $7.09 in federal taxes. Don pays $2.95 in state taxes. Don pays other taxes, too. His paycheck is for $66.61.

Shop Rite Food Store		1379
	Date	2/22/02
Amount SIXTY-SIX DOLLARS AND SIXTY-ONE CENTS		$66.61
PAY TO THE ORDER OF Don Park		
	Latisha Walker	

Don Park	1379
Pay Rate:	$10/hour
Hours:	8
Gross Pay:	$80

Deductions	
Federal Tax:	7.09
State Tax:	2.95
FICA:	1.58
Medicare:	1.77
Total Deductions	$13.39

B Circle.

1. The paycheck is for _____. (Don Park) Latisha Walker
2. Don makes _____. $8 an hour $10 an hour
3. Don works _____. 8 hours 10 hours
4. Don's federal taxes are _____. $2.95 $7.09
5. Don's state taxes are _____. $2.95 $7.09
6. Don's paycheck is for _____. $13.39 $66.61

C Write.

Don takes his check to the bank. He deposits $_____.

A) Read.

C.L.T. Human Resources   Employment application

Rodriguez	Sara	R.
LAST NAME	FIRST NAME	MI

5 Pine Street	San Francisco,	CA	94134
ADDRESS	CITY	STATE	ZIP

Telephone Number: (415) 555-9638

Work Experience: Cashier

Employer: Shop Rite Food Store

Years of Experience: 3

B) Complete the form.

C.L.T. Human Resources   Employment application

LAST NAME	FIRST NAME	MI

ADDRESS	CITY	STATE	ZIP

Telephone Number: (_ _ _) _ _ _ - _ _ _ _

Work Experience: _____

Employer: _____

Years of Experience: _____

10 Review

A Write the job.

cashier	cook	~~delivery person~~	receptionist	taxi driver

1. _delivery person_   2. _____   3. _____

4. _____   5. _____

B Listen and ✓ check the answer.

1. ✓ I'm a receptionist.   ___ I was a cashier.
2. ___ A computer.   ___ No, I don't.
3. ___ I'm a taxi driver.   ___ I was a taxi driver.
4. ___ I'm a gardener.   ___ Yes, I can.
5. ___ I can fix machines.   ___ I am a custodian.

C Community Challenge: Want ad

Find a want ad in a newspaper.

1. Job: _____

2. Address: _____

3. Phone number: _____

D Write *What* or *Where*.

1. A. _____What_____ is the phone number?
   B. 305-555-0099.

2. A. _____ is Family Restaurant?
   B. On Midway Avenue.

3. A. _____ do you do?
   B. I'm a cashier.

4. A. _____ do you live?
   B. Near the library.

5. A. _____ is your favorite color?
   B. Yellow.

E Learning Log

Write five words you remember.

Jobs	Job Activities	Paychecks
gardener	cooking	federal taxes

✓ Check what you can do.

1. I can talk about jobs.	___
2. I can say what my job was before.	___
3. I can understand a paycheck.	___
4. I can read want ads.	___
5. I can _____.	___

Looking Back

Talk about jobs on page 134. Now write three more words in your Learning Log.

How do you get to class?

What do you see?

A Listen.

1. take a bus

2. take a subway

3. ride a bike

4. drive a car

Listen and say.

B Listen.

Leo: How do you get to school?

Tien: I take a bus.

Listen and say.

C Talk with a partner.

A: How do you get to school?

B: I _____.

D Ask classmates.

You: How do you get to school?

Paul: I walk.

You: Please sign here.

WORD LIST

drive a car
ride a bike
take a bus
walk

walk	take a subway
name: _____	name: _____
take a bus	drive a car
name: _____	name: _____

A **Listen.**

1. on the left　　　**2.** straight ahead　　　**3.** on the right

Listen and say.

 B **Listen.**

Maria: Excuse me. Where is the movie theater?

Man: It's on the left.

Listen and say.

 C **Talk with a partner.**

A: Excuse me. Where is the _____?

B: It's _____.

  D **Listen and circle.**

1.	left	straight ahead	right
2.	left	straight ahead	right
3.	left	straight ahead	right
4.	left	straight ahead	right

A **Listen.**

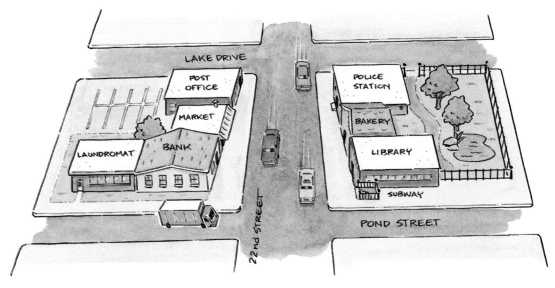

1. on the corner of   **2.** next to   **3.** between

Listen and say.

  B **Listen.**

Maria: Excuse me. Where is the post office?

Don: It's next to the market.

Listen and say.

 C **Talk with a partner.**

A: Excuse me. Where is the

_____?

B: It's next to the _____.

> ### WORD LIST
>
> laundromat/bank
> subway/library
> post office/market

149

A Match.

1. __C__ M-4 Bus   **a.** Northway Airport

2. ____ 108 Bus   **b.** Downtown Circle

3. ____ D Train   ~~c.~~ Westside Park

4. ____ Red Line   **d.** Brookline

B Listen.

Paul: How do I get to Northway Airport?

Sandy: Take the D Train.

Paul: The D Train? Thanks.

Listen and say.

C Talk with a partner.

A: How do I get to _____?

B: Take the _____.

A: The _____? Thanks.

WORD LIST

Oakland/C-6 Bus
Midway Airport/55 Bus
San Jose/B Train
Central Park/Yellow Line

A) Listen.

Carlos: When does the next train to Miami leave?

Woman: It leaves at 4:20.

Carlos: At 4:20? Thanks.

Listen and say.

B) Talk with a partner.

A: When does the next train to _____ leave?
(city)

B: It leaves at _____.
(time)

A: At _____? Thanks.
(time)

WORD LIST

Miami/4:20
New York/1:30
Seattle/8:45
Dallas/12:00

C) Listen and circle.

	Where?		When?	
1.	Cincinnati	(Chicago)	(6:14)	6:40
2.	Los Altos	Los Angeles	9:00	10:00
3.	San Diego	San Jose	2:00	12:00
4.	Newtown	Newark	10:02	10:12

(A) Listen and read.

Don wants to drive to school. He needs a learner's permit. Don needs to take a test to get his learner's permit. He calls to make an appointment. He can take the test on Thursday. The test is $25. After the test Leo can teach Don to drive.

(B) Circle.

1. Don needs _____. $25   ⟨a learner's permit⟩

2. He makes (a/an) _____.   appointment   test

3. His appointment is on _____. Tuesday   Thursday

4. The test is _____. $25   25¢

(C) Complete the form.

Application for a Learner's Permit

1. Name: _____

      (last)   (first)   (MI)

2. Date of birth: _____   5. ___ male ___ female

           (MM/DD/YY)

3. Eye color: _____   6. Hair color: _____

4. Glasses? ___ yes ___ no

                               _____

                               (signature)

male   female

A Listen.

1.

2.

3.

4.

5.

6.

H = Hospital

Listen and say.

B Write. Complete the road signs.

1.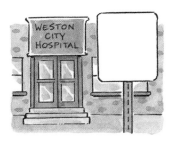

2.

C Circle the problem.

1.

a.

b.

2.

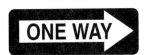

a.

b.

A Listen.

Carlos: How often does the B Train leave?

Isabel: It leaves every hour.

Carlos: Oh good. At 4:00, 5:00, and 6:00.

Listen and say.

B Listen.

Grace: How often does the 5 Bus leave?

Paul: It leaves every half hour.

Grace: Oh good. At 12:00, 12:30, and 1:00.

Listen and say.

C Listen.

Tien: How often does the subway leave?

Leo: It leaves every 15 minutes.

Tien: Oh good. At 10:15, 10:30, and 10:45.

Listen and say.

D Match.

1. ___	9:00	10:00	11:00	**a.**	every 15 minutes
2. ___	6:45	7:15	7:45	**b.**	every half hour
3. ___	3:30	3:45	4:00	**c.**	every hour

E Listen and circle.

1. Miami	every 15 minutes	every half hour	every hour
2. Chicago	every 15 minutes	every half hour	every hour
3. Dallas	every 15 minutes	every half hour	every hour

Reading a schedule

 A **Listen and read.**

This is a bus schedule for the K-52 Bus. It leaves Pond Street every 15 minutes. The bus goes to Westside Park, City Library, Weston School, and Northway Airport. It's 4:35. The next bus leaves Pond Street at 4:45.

B **Look at the bus schedule. Answer the questions.**

Bus K-52 leaves				
Pond Street	**Westside Park**	**City Library**	**Weston School**	**Northway Airport**
4:30	4:45	5:00	5:15	5:45
4:45	5:00	5:15	5:30	6:00
5:00	5:15	5:30	5:45	6:15
5:15	5:30	5:45	6:00	6:30
5:30	5:45	6:00	6:15	6:45

1. When does the bus leave Pond Street? _4:30, 4:45, 5:00, 5:15, and 5:30_ .

2. When does the bus leave Weston School? _____.

3. It's 5:10. When does the next bus leave City Library? _____.

4. It's 5:20. When does the next bus leave Weston School? _____.

5. It's 6:35. When does the next bus leave Northway Airport? _____.

A Listen and write.

A: Excuse me. _____ is the drugstore?

B: It's on the _____. Next to the movie theater.

B Listen and ✓ check.

1. ___ On the right.
2. ___ On the left.
3. ___ Straight ahead.
4. ___ It leaves at 2:00.
5. ___ Take the Blue Line.
6. ___ It leaves every 15 minutes.

✓ I take a subway.
___ I take a bus.
___ I walk.
___ Next to the drugstore.
___ It leaves at 10:20.
___ The Red Line stops here.

C Complete the road signs.

1.

2.

3.

4.
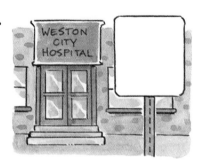

D **Write the letters in your name. Write words.**

Letters	Words
C	car
A	airport
R	right
L	left
O	on the corner of
S	subway

Letters	Words

E **Learning Log**

Write five words or phrases you remember.

Directions	Transportation	Road signs
straight ahead	bus	No Parking

✓ **Check what you can do.**

1. I can understand directions.	___
2. I can give directions.	___
3. I can understand road signs.	___
4. I can read a bus schedule.	___
5. I can _____.	___

 Looking Back

Look at page 146. What new words do you know? Write three more words in your Learning Log.

Grammar Spotlight for Units 10-12

A Can/Can't

I	can/can't	drive.
You		cook.
He		use a computer.
She		fix things.
It		walk.
We		speak Spanish.
They		ride bicycles.

Write *can* or *can't*.

1. Don has a learner's permit. He _____*can*_____ learn to drive now.

2. Carlos does not have a driver's license. He _____ be a taxi driver.

3. Don is a receptionist. He _____ use a computer.

4. Maria is from Mexico. She _____ speak Spanish.

5. Sandy has a fever. She _____ play basketball today.

6. Grace's hand hurts. She _____ write.

7. Tien is a delivery person. She _____ drive a car.

8. Paul is a custodian. He _____ fix things.

Complete with *next to* or *between*.

1. The drugstore is _____ the library.
2. The library is _____ the drugstore and the school.
3. The school is _____ the library.

 Complete the sentences with *in* or *on*.

1. Paul is _____ the library.
2. He has a bandage _____ his finger.
3. His book is _____ the table.
4. Paul lives _____ Los Angeles.
5. He lives _____ School Avenue.

A Match.

1. _c_ What's the matter?
2. ___ Can Dr. Green see my son today?
3. ___ What do you do?
4. ___ What was your job before?
5. ___ How do you get to school?
6. ___ Can you use a computer?
7. ___ How often does the train leave?

a. I was a cashier.
b. I'm a gardener.
c. I have a headache.
d. Yes, Dr. Green can see him.
e. It leaves every hour.
f. I take a bus.
g. Yes, I can.

B Listen. Complete.

a backache   ~~a cold~~   a headache   an infection   a toothache

Name	What's the matter?	When is the appointment?
1. Grace	a cold	11:00
2. Paul		
3. Tien		
4. Carlos		
5. Maria		

C What's the job?
Write the letters.

1. w <u>a</u> <u>i</u> <u>t</u> <u>e</u> <u>r</u>
2. c __ __ h i __ r
3. r __ c e __ t __ __ n __ s t
4. __ o __ k
5. d __ l i __ __ y p __ __ s __ n
6. __ u __ t o __ i a n
7. __ __ x __ d __ i __ __ r

D Community Challenge: Bus schedule

Bus	City	Leaves	City	Arrives
76	Los Angeles	6:00 a.m.	San Diego	10:00 a.m.
84	Los Angeles	7:15 a.m.	San Jose	5:00 p.m.
113	Los Angeles	9:00 a.m.	Oakland	7:25 p.m.
202	Los Angeles	11:00 a.m.	Las Vegas	4:45 p.m.
343	Los Angeles	11:45 p.m.	Sacramento	9:45 a.m.

Complete the sentences.

1. Bus _____84_____ leaves Los Angeles at _____.
   It arrives in San Jose at _____.
2. Bus _____343_____ leaves Los Angeles at _____.
   It arrives in _____ at ___9:45 a.m.___.
3. Bus _____113_____ leaves Los Angeles at _____.
   It arrives in _____ at _____.
4. Bus _____76_____ leaves Los Angeles at _____.
   It arrives in _____ at _____.
5. Bus _____ leaves Los Angeles at _____.
   It arrives in ___Las Vegas___ at _____.

Listening Script

Note: This listening script contains audio support for many of the activities in the Student Book. When the words on the Student Book page are identical to those on the audio program, a listening script is not provided.

Page 4

A. Listen.

A-B-C-D-E-F-G-H-I-J-K-L-M-N-O-
P-Q-R-S-T-U-V-W-X-Y-Z
Listen and say.

D. Listen and say the letters.
1. U-S-A
2. J-A-P-A-N
3. B-R-A-Z-I-L
4. M-E-X-I-C-O
5. V-I-E-T-N-A-M
6. T-H-A-I-L-A-N-D
7. C-O-L-O-M-B-I-A
8. V-E-N-E-Z-U-E-L-A

E. Listen and write.
1. n-a-m-e
2. h-e-l-l-o
3. f-r-o-m
4. w-r-i-t-e
5. y-o-u

Page 6

A. Listen.
1. student
2. paper
3. desk
4. chair
5. pen
6. board
7. backpack
8. computer
9. teacher
10. notebook
11. door
12. book

Page 8

A. Listen.
1. Open. Open the book.
2. Close. Close the book.
3. Put away. Put away the book.
4. Go to. Go to the board.
5. Take out. Take out the pen.
6. Point to. Point to the computer.
Listen and say.
1. open

2. close
3. put away
4. go to
5. take out
6. point to

B. Listen and circle.
1. Put away the paper.
2. Open the backpack.
3. Take out the book.

Page 9

A. Listen. Check what you hear.
1. Open the door.
2. Go to the board.
3. Take out the pen.
4. Put away the notebook.
5. Open the door.
6. Put away the paper.
7. Point to the desk.
8. Take out the book.

Page 10

A. Listen.
zero, one, two, three, four, five, six,
seven, eight, nine, ten
Listen and say.

E. Listen and circle.
1. Six.
2. Five.
3. Ten.
4. 5 Pen Avenue.
5. 555-5050.
6. 781-555-9876.

Page 12

A. Listen and write.
Sandy: <u>Hi</u>. I'm Sandy. What's your name?
Don: My <u>name</u> is Don.
Sandy: <u>Nice</u> to meet you, Don.
Don: Nice to <u>meet</u> you too, Sandy.

B. Listen and check the answer.
1. What's your name?
2. Nice to meet you.
3. What's your name?
4. How do you spell that?

5. What's this?
6. What's your phone number?

C. Listen and write.
Sandy: Hi. <u>I'm</u> Sandy. What's your name?
Grace: My <u>name</u> is Grace Lee.
Sandy: <u>How</u> do you spell that?
Grace: My <u>first</u> name is G-R-A-C-E.
My <u>last</u> name is L-E-E.

Page 18

A. Listen.
1. Married. Grace is married.
2. Single. Paul and Tlen are single.
3. Divorced. Leo is divorced.
4. Widowed. Maria is widowed.
Listen and say.
1. married
2. single
3. divorced
4. widowed

B. Listen and circle.
1. They are married.
2. He's widowed.
3. They are single.

Page 19

A. Listen.
Paul: I am average height. Leo is tall. Tien is short. Don and Carlos are average height.
Listen and say.
average height   tall   short

Page 21

B. Listen. Write the number.
1. He has brown hair and brown eyes. He's from Brazil.
2. He has white hair. He's divorced.
3. She is tall. She's Chinese.
4. She has red hair. She's from the USA.
5. She is widowed. She's from Mexico.
6. She is from Colombia. She speaks Spanish.

Page 24

A. Listen and write.
Grace: I am <u>tall</u>.
Leo: I <u>speak</u> Russian.
Tien: I wear <u>glasses</u>.
Isabel: I have <u>blond</u> hair. I have <u>blue</u> eyes.

B. Listen and check.
1. What language do you speak?
2. Who has red hair?
3. Where is Don from?
4. What's your zip code?

Page 27

A. Listen.
1. Mother. This is Sandy's mother.
2. Father. This is Sandy's father.
3. Brother. This is Sandy's brother.
4. Husband. This is Sandy's husband.
5. Daughter. This is Sandy's daughter.
6. Sons. These are Sandy's sons.

Listen and say.
1. mother
2. father
3. brother
4. husband
5. daughter
6. sons

Page 28

A. Listen.
Sandy: This is my father, Arthur.
This is my mother, Ann.
This is my brother, John.
This is my sister-in-law, Tomiko.
This is my husband, Will.
This is my niece, Mary.
These are my sons, Andy and Justin.
This is my daughter, Alexandra.

Listen and say.
father, mother, brother, sister-in-law, husband, niece, sons, daughter

B. Listen and write.
1. Justin is Sandy's <u>son</u>.
2. Alexandra is Sandy's <u>daughter</u>.
3. John is Sandy's <u>brother</u>.
4. Will is Sandy's <u>husband</u>.
5. Arthur is Sandy's <u>father</u>.
6. Ann is Sandy's <u>mother</u>.

7. Tomiko is Sandy's <u>sister-in-law</u>.
8. Mary is Sandy's <u>niece</u>.

Page 36

A. Listen and write.
1. My name is <u>Ms.</u> Redman.
2. I live at <u>60</u> Brown Road.
3. I am <u>married</u>.
4. My husband's <u>name</u> is Bill.
5. We have five <u>children</u>.
6. My <u>sister</u> has five children, too.

B. Listen and check the answer.
1. How old are you?
2. Do you have children?
3. Is she married?
4. Who is Andy?
5. Who is Ann?

C. Listen and circle.
1. eighty
2. sixty
3. nineteen
4. twenty-five
5. seventeen
6. twelve
7. fourteen
8. fifty

Page 40

B. Listen and check.
1. Mary is young. She has red hair. She is single.
2. Peter is old. He has white hair. He is single.
3. Anna is young. She has black hair. She is married.

Page 43

A. Listen.
1. Kitchen. This is the kitchen.
2. Living room. This is the living room.
3. Bedroom. This is the the bedroom.
4. Dining room. This is the dining room.
5. Bathroom. This is the bathroom.
6. Yard. This is the yard.

Listen and say.
1. kitchen
2. living room

3. bedroom
4. dining room
5. bathroom
6. yard

Page 44

A. Listen.
1. Table. Is there a table in the dining room?
2. Sofa. Is there a sofa in the living room?
3. Bed. Is there a bed in the bedroom?
4. Lamp. Is there a lamp in the bedroom?
5. CD player. Is there a CD player in the living room?
6. Fireplace. Is there a fireplace in the living room?
7. Dresser. Is there a dresser in the bedroom?
8. Rug. Is there a rug in the bedroom?

Listen and say.
1. table
2. sofa
3. bed
4. lamp
5. CD player
6. fireplace
7. dresser
8. rug

Page 45

A. Listen.
1. Shower. This is a shower.
2. Hall. This is a hall.
3. Sink. This is a sink.
4. Stove. This is a stove.
5. Window. This is a window.
6. Microwave oven. This is a microwave oven.
7. Closet. This is a closet.
8. Refrigerator. This is a refrigerator.
9. Tub. This is a tub.
10. Barbecue. This is a barbecue.

Listen and say.
1. shower
2. hall
3. sink
4. stove
5. window

6. microwave oven
7. closet
8. refrigerator
9. tub
10. barbecue

B. Listen and circle.
1. There's a tub in the bathroom.
2. There's a barbecue in the yard.
3. There's a sink in the kitchen.
4. There's a closet in the bedroom.
5. There's a window in the dining room.
6. There's a refrigerator in the kitchen.

Page 48

A. Listen and circle.
1. There's a stove in the kitchen.
2. There's a sofa in the living room.
3. There's a barbecue in the yard.
4. There's a table in the dining room.

Page 49

A. Listen.
1. In the city. Leo's dream house is in the city.
2. In the country. Isabel's dream house is in the country.
3. At the beach. Paul's dream house is at the beach.
4. In the suburbs. Don's dream house is in the suburbs.

Listen and say.
1. in the city
2. in the country
3. at the beach
4. in the suburbs

Page 50

A. Listen.
1. twelve   twenty
2. thirteen   thirty
3. fourteen   forty
4. fifteen   fifty
5. sixteen   sixty
6. seventeen   seventy
7. eighteen   eighty
8. nineteen   ninety

Listen and say.

B. Listen and circle.
1. sixteen
2. nineteen

3. forty
4. eighteen
5. thirteen
6. seventy
7. twelve
8. fifty

C. Listen and write.
1. My address is 50 Beach Street.
2. The house is 70 years old.
3. The rented room is at 20 Hall Road.
4. There are 13 apartments.
5. There are 19 windows.
6. I have 12 tables.
7. We need 40 chairs in the dining room.
8. He has 14 pens.
9. The house has 18 rooms.
10. There are 17 lamps in the garage.

Page 51

B. Listen and match.
Sandy's students are at a garage sale. What do they need?
1. Isabel needs a lamp.
2. Carlos needs a backpack.
3. Don needs some CDs.
4. Maria needs a bike.

Page 52

A. Listen and circle.
1. There is a sink in the bathroom.
2. There are books in the bedroom.
3. Paul lives in the suburbs.
4. Tomiko is 30.

B. Listen and check.
1. Where is Maria?
2. Is there a lamp in the living room?
3. What do you need?
4. Do you need a dresser?

Page 55

B. Listen and circle.
1. **Sandy:** What do you do every day, Leo?
   Leo: I read the newspaper.
2. **Sandy:** What do you do every day, Paul?
   Paul: I brush my teeth.
3. **Sandy:** What do you do every day, Carlos?
   Carlos: I watch TV.

4. **Sandy:** What do you do every day, Maria?
   Maria: I eat breakfast.

Page 56

A. Listen.
Sunday Monday Tuesday
Wednesday Thursday Friday
Saturday
Listen and say.

B. Listen and circle.
1. My sisters study on Monday.
2. My brothers cook dinner on Thursday.
3. I go to garage sales on Sunday.
4. Paul and Leo play basketball on Saturday.

C. Listen and write.
1. I play soccer on Thursday.
2. We go to my mother's house on Friday.
3. My nieces go to garage sales on Saturday.
4. I go to class on Monday.
5. I cook dinner on Tuesday.
6. Grace and I study on Wednesday.

Page 57

A. Listen.
January February March April
May June July August
September October November
December
Listen and say.

Page 58

A. Listen.
1. Ten o'clock. It's ten o'clock.
2. Seven fifteen. It's seven fifteen.
3. One forty-five. It's one forty-five.
4. Three thirty. It's three thirty.
5. Two o'clock. It's two o'clock.
6. Four forty-five. It's four forty-five.
7. Twelve thirty. It's twelve thirty.
8. Eight fifteen. It's eight fifteen.

Listen and say.
1. ten o'clock
2. seven fifteen
3. one forty-five
4. three thirty
5. two o'clock

164

6. four forty-five
7. twelve thirty
8. eight fifteen

Page 59

A. Listen.
1. Six o'clock. It's six o'clock.
2. Eight fifteen. It's eight fifteen.
3. Three thirty. It's three thirty.
4. Five forty-five. It's five forty-five.
Listen and say.
1. six o'clock
2. eight fifteen
3. three thirty
4. five forty-five

B. Listen and circle.
1. It's seven thirty.
2. She eats breakfast at eight thirty.
3. She goes to school at twelve forty-five.
4. They study at two fifteen.
5. Carlos reads the newspaper at four o'clock.
6. He goes to sleep at nine fifteen.

Page 60

C. Listen and write the times.
Grace: I'd like to make an appointment for a haircut.
Man: Can you come on Monday at five thirty?
Grace: Monday at five thirty? That's fine.
Grace: I'd like to make an appointment for a tune-up.
Woman: Can you come on Wednesday at three o'clock?
Grace: Wednesday at three o'clock? That's fine.
Grace: I'd like to make an appointment for a cleaning.
Man: Can you come on Friday at one fifteen?
Grace: Friday at one fifteen? That's fine.

Page 62

C. Listen and circle.
1. Paul lives on Fifth Street.
2. Tien lives on Third Avenue.
3. Go to Twelfth Street.

4. The garage sale is on Fourteenth Street.
5. I live on Thirteenth Street.
6. Grace lives on First Avenue.

D. Listen.
Woman: What is your date of birth?
Grace: March sixteenth, 1964.
Listen and say.

Page 64

A. Listen and write.
1. My birthday is <u>October</u> twelfth.
2. Paul's birthday is <u>July</u> fourth.
3. My class is at <u>four thirty</u>.
4. I study on <u>Tuesday</u>.

B. Listen and check the answer.
1. How often do you shop for food?
2. When do you go to garage sales?
3. What do you do every day?
4. What time is it?
5. Can you come on Sunday at five o'clock ?
6. What is your date of birth?

C. Listen and circle.
1. Can you come at seven o'clock?
2. He lives on Sixth Street.
3. The house is on Eleventh Street.
4. I go to school at two thirty.
5. My birthday is May thirteenth.
6. I go to school at nine forty-five.

Page 65

D. Listen and write.
Cleaning Appointment
On <u>Monday</u>, <u>April</u> 21st at <u>eight a.m.</u>
Edward J. Weiss, D.D.S.
517 Old Road
Santa Cruz, California

Jane's Haircuts
Hours
Tuesday to Saturday
nine thirty a.m. to <u>six p.m.</u>
310 Cook Road
Middletown, Michigan

Page 67

A. Listen.
1. A shirt. Don is looking for a shirt.
2. A coat. Maria is looking for a coat.

3. A sweater. Isabel is looking for a sweater.
4. Shoes. Grace is looking for shoes.
5. A watch. Leo is looking for a watch.
6. A dress. Maria is looking for a dress.
7. Pants. Don is looking for pants.
8. A suit. Paul is looking for a suit.
Listen and say.
1. a shirt
2. a coat
3. a sweater
4. shoes
5. a watch
6. a dress
7. pants
8. a suit

Page 68

A. Listen
1. A blouse. Isabel is looking for a blouse.
2. A bathing suit. Carlos is looking for a bathing suit.
3. A skirt. Grace is looking for a skirt.
4. A jacket. Paul is looking for a jacket.
5. Sneakers. Leo is looking for sneakers.
Listen and say.
1. a blouse
2. a bathing suit
3. a skirt
4. a jacket
5. sneakers

Page 69

B. Listen and circle.
1. yellow sneakers
2. a blue sweater
3. a green blouse
4. a purple jacket
5. a pink bathing suit
6. a black skirt

Page 72

A. Listen.
1. Small. The red shirt is small.
2. Medium. The blue shirt is medium.

3. Large. The green shirt is large.

Listen and say.
1. small
2. medium
3. large

C. Listen and circle.
1. Paul is a large.
2. Tien is a small.
3. Carlos is a large.
4. Isabel is a medium.

Page 73

A. Listen.
1. Too short. The pants are too short.
2. Too long. The sweater is too long.
3. Too small. The jacket is too small.
4. Too big. The blouse is too big.

Listen and say.
1. too short
2. too long
3. too small
4. too big

Page 74

A. Listen.
1. A penny. One cent.
2. A nickel. Five cents.
3. A dime. Ten cents.
4. A quarter. Twenty-five cents.

Listen and say.
1. A penny. One cent.
2. A nickel. Five cents.
3. A dime. Ten cents.
4. A quarter. Twenty-five cents.

B. Listen.
1. One dollar.
2. Five dollars.
3. Ten dollars.
4. Twenty dollars.

Listen and say.
1. One dollar.
2. Five dollars.
3. Ten dollars.
4. Twenty dollars.

Page 76

B. Listen and check.
1. What size are you?
2. May I help you?

3. What is he wearing?
4. What is your favorite color?

Page 83

A. Listen.
1. Eggs. We need eggs.
2. Ice cream. We need ice cream.
3. Carrots. We need carrots.
4. Apples. We need apples.
5. Potatoes. We need potatoes.
6. Milk. We need milk.

Listen and say.
1. eggs
2. ice cream
3. carrots
4. apples
5. potatoes
6. milk

Page 84

A. Listen.
1. Cake. Do we need cake?
2. Bread. Do we need bread?
3. Beef. Do we need beef?
4. Chicken. Do we need chicken?
5. Oranges. Do we need oranges?
6. Butter. Do we need butter?
7. Cheese. Do we need cheese?

Listen and say.
1. cake
2. bread
3. beef
4. chicken
5. oranges
6. butter
7. cheese

Page 85

B. Listen and complete the chart.
1. Apples are in Aisle 1.
2. Beef is in Aisle 2.
3. Chicken is in Aisle 2.
4. Cheese is in Aisle 4.
5. Cake is in Aisle 3.
6. Oranges are in Aisle 1.
7. Milk is in Aisle 4.

Page 86

A. Listen.
1. Breakfast. At seven o'clock, I eat breakfast.
2. Lunch. At twelve thirty, I eat lunch.

3. Dinner. At six forty-five, I eat dinner.

Listen and say.
1. breakfast
2. lunch
3. dinner

Page 88

A. Listen.
Pizza
Tuna sandwich
Hamburger
Cherry pie
Coffee
Tea
Soda
Listen and say.

Page 90

A. Listen.
1. A bottle. This is a bottle of oil.
2. A can. This is a can of tomato soup.
3. A bag. This is a bag of rice.
4. A package. This is a package of sugar.
5. A box. This is a box of cereal.
6. A bunch. This is a bunch of grapes.
7. A jar. This is a jar of peanut butter.

Listen and say.
1. a bottle
2. a can
3. a bag
4. a package
5. a box
6. a bunch
7. a jar

B. Listen and circle.
1. I need a bunch of grapes.
2. We need a bag of rice.
3. Do we need a can of soup?
4. They need a package of sugar.
5. She needs a box of cereal.
6. Paul needs a bottle of oil.

Page 92

A. Listen and check the food Maria needs to buy.
1. I need to buy chicken.
2. I need milk for breakfast.
3. I need apples for lunch.

4. I need oranges, too.

5. I need cheese.

B. Listen and circle the answer.

1. Where's the bread?

2. What do you usually have for breakfast?

3. Excuse me. Where are the oranges?

4. What do we need?

5. May I help you?

6. Anything else?

Page 95

A. Listen.

1. Sunny. It's sunny.

2. Snowy. It's snowy.

3. Hot. It's hot.

4. Cold. It's cold.

5. Windy. It's windy.

6. Rainy. It's rainy.

Listen and say.

1. It's sunny.

2. It's snowy.

3. It's hot.

4. It's cold.

5. It's windy.

6. It's rainy.

Page96

A. Listen and circle.

1. It's rainy.

2. It's hot.

3. It's cold.

4. It's windy.

Page 97

A. Listen.

1. Winter. It's winter.

2. Spring. It's spring.

3. Summer. It's summer.

4. Fall. It's fall.

Listen and say.

1. winter

2. spring

3. summer

4. fall

Page 98

A. Listen.

1. Walking. She's walking.

2. Playing soccer. He's playing soccer.

3. Dancing. They're dancing.

4. Reading. She's reading.

5. Swimming. He's swimming.

6. Listening to music. She's listening to music.

7. Cooking. He's cooking.

8. Watching TV. He's watching TV.

Listen and say.

1. walking

2. playing soccer

3. dancing

4. reading

5. swimming

6. listening to music

7. cooking

8. watching TV

Page 99

A. Listen and circle.

1. He's eating ice cream.

2. She's reading.

3. They're dancing.

4. He's swimming.

Page 102

A. Listen and write the numbers.

1. It's very hot. It's 105 degrees Fahrenheit.

2. It's hot. It's 85 degrees Fahrenheit.

3. It's cool. It's 50 degrees Fahrenheit.

4. It's cold. It's 27 degrees Fahrenheit.

Page 104

A. Listen and write.

1. How's the <u>weather</u>?

2. It's <u>cold</u>.

3. My favorite season is <u>fall</u>.

4. I'm <u>playing</u> soccer.

5. What are you <u>doing</u>?

6. They like <u>reading</u>.

B. Listen and check.

1. How's the weather?

2. How's the weather in New York?

3. What's your favorite season?

4. What are you doing?

5. What's Maria doing?

6. What do you like doing in the fall?

C. Listen and circle.

1. It's 60 degrees Fahrenheit.

2. Seattle is windy.

3. It's 55 degrees Fahrenheit in Miami.

4. Dallas is 40 degrees Fahrenheit.

5. It's cold in New York.

6. Los Angeles is rainy.

Page 107

A. Listen. Look at page 106.

1. Police station. I'm going to the police station.

2. Bank. I'm going to the bank.

3. Drugstore. I'm going to the drugstore.

4. Hospital. I'm going to the hospital.

5. Fire station. I'm going to the fire station.

6. Gas station. I'm going to the gas station.

7. Library. I'm going to the library.

8. Post office. I'm going to the post office.

Listen and say.

1. police station

2. bank

3. drugstore

4. hospital

5. fire station

6. gas station

7. library

8. post office

Page 111

A. Listen and write.

1. The gas station is <u>next to</u> the library.

2. The hospital is <u>between</u> the gas station and the bank.

3. The hospital is <u>on</u> 19th Street.

4. The police station is <u>next to</u> the hospital.

5. The post office is <u>between</u> the library and the hospital.

6. Don and Sumin are <u>in</u> the bank.

7. Leo is <u>in</u> the drugstore.

8. The gas station is <u>on</u> South Avenue.

Page 112

A. Listen.

1. Near. He's near the bus stop.

167

2. Far from. He's far from the bus stop.

Listen and say.
1. He's near the bus stop.
2. He's far from the bus stop.

B. Listen and circle.
1. The man lives near a bank.
2. She lives near a bus stop.
3. Sandy lives far from the city.
4. Paul lives near a fire station.
5. We live far from a movie theater.
6. Tien lives near a post office.

Page 113

A. Listen.
1. See a movie. Where do you see a movie?
2. Buy stamps. Where do you buy stamps?
3. Wash clothes. Where do you wash clothes?
4. Make a deposit. Where do you make a deposit?

Listen and say.
1. see a movie
2. buy stamps
3. wash clothes
4. make a deposit

Page 115

A. Listen and read.
Don is taking money from his checking account. He's making a withdrawal.
1. Insert your ATM card.
2. Enter your PIN. Press Enter.
3. Pick one: Withdrawal, Deposit, Balance.
4. Pick one. Savings, Checking, Credit.
5. Pick one: twenty dollars, forty dollars, sixty dollars, one hundred dollars, two hundred dollars.
6. Please take your money.

Page 116

A. Listen and write.
Isabel: <u>Excuse</u> me. Where is the police station?
Man: It's <u>on</u> 54th Street.
Isabel: <u>Thanks</u>.

B. Listen and check.
1. Where are you going?
2. Where's the bank?
3. Where's the library?
4. Do you live near a movie theater?

C. Listen and write.
1.
Waiter: Can I help you?
Sandy: Yes. I'll have a tuna sandwich.
2.
Leo: This is a good movie.
Paul: Yes, it is.
3.
Teller: May I help you?
Grace: I want to make a deposit, please.
4.
Clerk: Good morning.
Don: Good morning. I want to buy some stamps.

Page 120

B. Listen and circle the correct answer.
1.
Mother: Hello?
Isabel: Hi Mother. It's Isabel. How are you?
Mother: Hi Isabel. How's the weather in Los Angeles?
Isabel: It's rainy.
2.
Grace: Hi, Maria.
Maria: Hi, Grace.
Grace: What are Carlos and Tien doing?
Maria: They're playing soccer.
3.
Isabel: Hello?
Don: Hi Isabel.
Isabel: Hi, Don. How's the weather in Miami?
Don: It's cloudy.

Page 123

A. Listen.
1. An earache. I have an earache.
2. A sore throat. I have a sore throat.
3. A headache. I have a headache.

4. A broken arm. I have a broken arm.
5. A toothache. I have a toothache.
6. A stomachache. I have a stomachache.
7. A backache. I have a backache.
8. A cold. I have a cold.

Listen and say.
1. an earache
2. a sore throat
3. a headache
4. a broken arm
5. a toothache
6. a stomachache
7. a backache
8. a cold

Page 126

C. Listen and check.
1. Isabel
Isabel: Ow! I have a cut on my hand.
Dr. Brown: You need a bandage.
2. Carlos
Carlos: I have a fever.
Dr. Brown: You need aspirin.
3. Don
Don: Ow! My foot hurts. I have an infection.
Dr. Brown: You need an antibiotic.
4. Leo
Leo: Oh, my head is hot. I feel bad. I have a fever.
Dr. Brown: Oh, no. You need aspirin.

Page 127

C. Listen. Complete the chart.
1. Leo
Grace: What's the matter, Leo?
Leo: I have a cut on my finger.
Grace: That's too bad. You need a bandage.
2. Isabel
Carlos: What's the matter, Isabel?
Isabel: I have a headache. My head hurts.
Carlos: That's too bad. You need aspirin.
3. Paul
Leo: What's the matter, Paul?
Paul: I have an infection. My foot hurts.

Grace: That's too bad. You need an antibiotic.

Page 128

A. Listen.
1. Exercise. I exercise.
2. Drink water. I drink water.
3. Get enough sleep. I get enough sleep.
4. Eat healthy food. I eat healthy food.

Listen and say.
1. exercise
2. drink water
3. get enough sleep
4. eat healthy food

D. Listen and follow the directions.
Look at your teacher.
1. Stand up.
2. Raise your arms.
3. Stretch.
4. Touch your toes.
5. Jump.
6. Touch your toes.
7. Jump.
8. Stretch.
9. Raise your arms.
10. Sit down.

Page 132

B. Listen and check.
1. What's the matter?
2. What's the matter with Don?
3. Can Dr. Wall see me today?
4. What's the matter with Sandy?

Page 135

A. Listen. Look at page 134.
1. A custodian. She's a custodian.
2. A delivery person. He's a delivery person.
3. A receptionist. He's a receptionist.
4. A taxi driver. She's a taxi driver.
5. A cashier. He's a cashier.
6. A cook. He's a cook.
7. A waiter. He's a waiter.
8. A gardener. He's a gardener.

Listen and say.
1. a custodian
2. a delivery person
3. a receptionist
4. a taxi driver

5. a cashier
6. a cook
7. a waiter
8. a gardener

Page 136

A. Listen.
1. A taxi cab. A taxi driver drives a taxi cab.
2. Pots and pans. A cook uses pots and pans.
3. A computer. A receptionist uses a computer.
4. A cash register. A cashier uses a cash register.

Listen and say.
1. a taxi cab
2. pots and pans
3. a computer
4. a cash register

C. Listen and circle.
1. **Woman:** I am a receptionist. I use a computer.
2. **Man:** I am a cook. I use pots and pans.
3. **Man:** I am a taxi driver. I drive a taxi cab.
4. **Woman:** I am a cashier. I use a cash register.

Page 137

A. Listen.
1. Indoors. Do you like to work indoors?
2. Outdoors. Do you like to work outdoors?
3. With people. Do you like to work with people?
4. With machines. Do you like to work with machines?

Listen and say.
1. indoors
2. outdoors
3. with people
4. with machines

Page 138

A. Listen.
1. Drive. I can drive a car.
2. Fix. I can fix things.
3. Use. I can use a computer.
4. Sell. I can sell things.

Listen and say.
1. drive
2. fix
3. use
4. sell

Page 140

C. Listen and check the ad from Activity A.
1. My name is Sara Holt. I am a cashier. I want to work at Wilder Men's Shop.
2. Hi, I'm Ben Lee. I want the custodian job. I can fix things.
3. My name is Frank Jones. I live in San Diego. I'm a good custodian.
4. Hi, I'm John Miller. I like to work with people. I'm a good cashier.

Page 144

B. Listen and check the answer.
1. What do you do?
2. Do you like to work with machines?
3. What was your job before?
4. Can you drive a car?
5. What can you do?

Page 147

A. Listen.
1. Take a bus. I take a bus.
2. Take a subway. I take a subway.
3. Ride a bike. I ride a bike.
4. Drive a car. I drive a car.

Listen and say.
1. take a bus
2. take a subway
3. ride a bike
4. drive a car

Page 148

A. Listen
1. On the left. The movie theater is on the left.
2. Straight ahead. The post office is straight ahead.
3. On the right. The bank is on the right.

Listen and say.
1. on the left
2. straight ahead
3. on the right

D. Listen and circle.
1. The bank is on the right.
2. The post office is straight ahead.
3. The movie theater is on the left.
4. The drugstore is on the right.

Page 149

A. Listen.
1. On the corner of. The bank is on the corner of 22nd Street and Pond Street.
2. Next to. The laundromat is next to the bank.
3. Between. The market is between the bank and the post office.

Listen and say.
1. on the corner of
2. next to
3. between

Page 151

C. Listen and circle.
1.
Man: When does the next train to Chicago leave?
Woman: It leaves at six fourteen.
Man: At six fourteen? Thanks.
2.
Man: When does the next train to Los Altos leave?
Woman: It leaves at ten o'clock.
Man: At ten o'clock? Thanks.
3.
Woman: When does the next train to San Diego leave?
Man: It leaves at twelve o'clock.
Woman: At twelve o'clock? Thanks.
4.
Woman: When does the next train to Newark leave?
Man: It leaves at ten oh two.
Woman: At ten oh two? Thanks.

Page 153

A. Listen.
1. Bus Stop
2. Speed Limit thirty-five
3. Stop
4. One Way
5. Hospital
6. No Parking Any Time

Listen and say.

Page 154

E. Listen and circle.
1. Miami
Man: When does the bus to Miami leave?
Woman: It leaves every half hour.
2. Chicago
Man: When does the train to Chicago leave?
Woman: It leaves every 15 minutes.
3. Dallas
Man: When does the train to Dallas leave?
Woman: It leaves every hour.

Page 156

A. Listen and write.
A: Excuse me. <u>Where</u> is the drugstore?
B: It's on the <u>left</u>. Next to the movie theater.

B. Listen and check.
1. How do you get to work?
2. How do you get to school?
3. Excuse me. Where is the police station?
4. When does the next bus to Portland leave?
5. Excuse me. How do I get to Central Park?
6. How often does the train leave?

Page 160

B. Listen. Complete.
1. Grace
Grace: Hello. This is Grace Lee. I have a cold. Can Dr. Brown see me today?
Woman: Dr. Brown can see you at eleven o'clock.
Grace: At eleven o'clock? That's fine. Thank you.
2. Paul
Paul: This is Paul Lemat. I have a headache. Can the doctor see me today?
Woman: Yes. Dr. Brown can see you at three thirty this afternoon.
Paul: At three thirty? Thank you.
3. Tien
Tien: Hello. This is Tien Lam. I have

a toothache. Can I see Dr. Green today?
Woman: Dr. Green can see you at twelve thirty.
Tien: At twelve thirty? Fine.
4. Carlos
Carlos: This is Carlos Avila. I have an infection.
Woman: Can you come at four fifteen?
Carlos: Four fifteen? Yes, I can be there at four fifteen.
5. Maria
Maria: Hello. This is Maria Cruz. I have a backache. Can I see Dr. Brown today?
Woman: Dr. Brown can see you at one forty-five.
Maria: At one forty-five? That's fine. Thank you.

Vocabulary List

Unit 1

address
backpack
board
book
chair
check
circle
close
complete
computer
desk
door
eight
e-mail address
Emergency
    Information Form
first name
five
four
go to
hello
hi
last name
match
name
nine
notebook
one
open
paper
pen
phone number
point to
put away
seven
six
spell
student
take out
teacher
ten
three
two
zero

Unit 2

address
average height
black
blond
blue

Brazil
brown
China
Chinese
Colombia
divorced
eighteen
eleven
Identification Form
eyes
fifteen
fourteen
from
glasses
green
hair
Korea
Korean
language
married
Mexico
nineteen
Portuguese
red
Russia
Russian
seventeen
short
single
sixteen
Spanish
speak
tall
thirteen
twelve
Vietnam
Vietnamese
wear
white
widowed
zip code

Unit 3

aunt
brother
census form
children
daughter
eighty
family
father
fifty
forty

granddaughter
grandfather
grandmother
husband
middle-aged
mother
Mr.
Mrs.
Ms.
niece
ninety
old
one hundred
parent
seventy
sister
sister-in-law
sixty
son
thirty
twenty
uncle
young

Unit 4

apartment
barbecue
bathroom
beach
bed
bedroom
bike
CD player
city
closet
cook
country
dining room
dream house
dresser
eat
fireplace
furniture
garage sale
hall
home
house
kitchen
lamp
live
living room
microwave oven
need

pan
refrigerator
rented room
rug
sale
shower
sink
sleep
sofa
stove
study
suburbs
table
toaster
tub
window
yard

Unit 5

appointment
April
August
basketball
birthday
breakfast
brush
cleaning
clock
computer
date of birth
day
December
dinner
eat
eighth
eleventh
English
every day
February
fifth
first
fourteenth
fourth
Friday
haircut
home
January
July
June
make
March
May
Monday

movie
newspaper
ninth
November
o'clock
October
often
once a month
once a week
people
phone
play
read
Saturday
second
September
seventh
sixth
start
Sunday
talk
teeth
tenth
third
thirteenth
Thursday
time
Tuesday
tune-up
TV
twelfth
watch
Wednesday
week
work

Unit 6

bathing suit
big
black
blouse
blue
brown
cent
coat
color
dime
dollar
dress
favorite
green
help
jacket

171

large
long
medium
money
nickel
pants
penny
pink
purple
quarter
red
shirt
shoes
short
size
skirt
small
sneakers
suit
sweater
watch
wear
white
yellow

Unit 7

aisle
apples
bakery
bag
bananas
beef
bottle
box
break
breakfast
bunch
butter
cake
can
carrots
cereal
cheese
chicken
dairy
dinner
eggs
excuse me
food
fruit
hamburger
hungry
ice cream

jar
lunch
meat
milk
need
oranges
orange juice
package
pizza
potatoes
potluck dinner
tuna sandwich
usually
vegetables

Unit 8

basketball
Celsius
cloudy
cold
cook
cool
dance
degrees
fall
Fahrenheit
favorite
hot
listen
map
music
play
rainy
read
season
snowy
soccer
spring
summer
sunny
swim
temperature
walk
watch
weather
weather map
windy
winter

Unit 9

ATM
bank
between

bus stop
buy stamps
checking account
deposit
drugstore
excuse me
far from
fire station
gas station
hospital
in
laundromat
library
make a deposit
movie theater
near
neighborhood
next to
on
park
police station
post office
restaurant
savings account
supermarket
thanks
wash clothes
watch a movie
withdrawal

Unit 10

antibiotic
arm
aspirin
backache
bandage
broken arm
capsule
cold
co-payment
cough
cough syrup
cut
drink water
earache
eat
exercise
eye
fever
finger
foot
hand
head

headache
health insurance
healthy
hurt
infection
jump
leg
medicine
nose
once
pill
raise
sick
sleep
sore throat
stomach
stomachache
stretch
three times
toes
toothache
touch
twice

Unit 11

cash register
cashier
computer
cook
custodian
delivery person
drive
employer
fix
gardener
indoors
job application
machines
outdoors
pan
paycheck
people
pot
receptionist
sell
taxi cab
taxi driver
use
waiter
want ad
work

Unit 12

airport
between
bike
bus
car
drive
hospital
learner's permit
leave
left
next to
no parking
on the corner of
one way
ride
right
road sign
schedule
speed limit
stop
straight ahead
subway
take

Index

BASIC SKILLS

Alphabet: 4, 5, 6

Listening: 3, 4, 5, 6. 8. 9. 10, 12, 15, 16, 17, 18, 21, 22, 24, 27, 28, 29, 30, 31, 33, 34, 35, 36, 40, 43, 44, 45, 46, 47, 48, 49, 50, 51, 52, 55, 56, 57, 58, 59, 60, 61, 62, 63, 64, 65, 67, 68, 69, 70, 71, 72, 73, 74, 75, 76, 83, 84, 85, 87, 88, 89, 90, 91, 92, 95, 96, 97, 98, 99, 100, 101, 102, 104, 106, 108, 109, 110, 111, 112, 113, 114, 115, 116, 120, 123, 124, 125, 126, 127, 128, 129, 130, 131, 132, 135, 136, 137, 139, 140, 141, 143, 144, 147, 148, 149, 150, 151, 152, 153, 156, 160

Speaking: 3, 4, 5, 6, 9, 15, 16, 17, 27, 29, 30, 31, 43, 44, 46, 47, 51, 55, 56, 58, 61, 65, 67, 68, 69, 70, 71, 72, 74, 80, 83, 84, 85, 86, 88, 89, 91, 92, 93, 95, 97, 98, 99, 100, 105, 106, 108, 109, 110, 112, 113, 116, 121, 123, 124, 125, 126, 127, 128, 130, 135, 137, 139, 141, 147, 148, 149, 150, 151

Reading: 3, 7, 11, 23, 29, 31, 33, 35, 47, 49, 59, 60, 61, 63, 75, 81, 91, 101, 114, 129, 131, 140, 141, 152, 155

Writing: 4, 6, 10, 11, 12, 13, 16, 19, 20, 21, 22, 24, 25, 28, 32, 34, 37, 46, 49, 50, 56, 57, 62, 63, 65, 68, 73, 75, 81, 89, 101, 103, 104, 111, 113, 114, 115, 118, 119, 129, 132, 138, 141, 143, 144, 145, 150, 153, 157, 161

GRAMMAR

articles "a", "an": 78

"Be" with negatives: 39

"can," "can't": 158

imperatives: 8, 9

negative sentences: 59

prepositions: 111, 159

present continuous tense: 118

pronouns: 38

simple present tense: 38, 39, 79

singular and plural nouns: 78

LEARNING STRATEGIES

Abilities ("can do"): 13, 25, 37, 53, 65, 77, 93, 105, 117, 133, 145, 157

Games: 5, 24, 41, 52, 64, 76, 89, 116, 127

Group Work (with class): 9, 11, 15, 16, 17, 29, 30, 31, 46, 57, 58, 62, 71, 86, 89, 91, 92, 100, 105, 112, 139, 147

Pair Work (with partner): 3, 5, 6, 9, 10, 19, 27, 30, 31, 34, 43, 44, 46, 47, 51, 55, 61, 67, 68, 69, 70, 71, 72, 74, 80, 83, 84, 85, 86, 88, 89, 93, 95, 97, 98, 99, 100, 106, 108, 109, 110, 113, 115, 121, 123, 124, 125, 127, 135, 137, 139, 141, 147, 148, 149, 150, 151

True/False: 81, 91

Learning Logs: 13, 25, 37, 53, 65, 77, 93, 105, 117, 133, 145, 157

SUPPORTING SKILLS

Alphabet: 4, 5, 6

Completing Charts: 16, 17, 37, 85, 103

Completing Forms: emergency 11; identification 23; census 35; health 63, 131; application 153

Completing Sentences: 7, 9, 12, 20, 22, 36, 45, 49, 52, 56, 87, 97, 111, 116, 119, 130, 138, 145, 161

Finding "wrong word": 113

Matching: 7, 21, 40, 51, 67, 73, 74, 76, 80, 96, 106, 119, 120, 140, 150, 160

Questions and answers: 5, 6, 11

Spelling: 11

TOPICS

CLOTHING
Colors: 69, 71
Kinds of clothing: 66, 67, 68, 78, 81
Sizes: 72, 73, 76, 81

COMMUNITY RESOURCES
Department of Motor Vehicles: 41, 152
Emergencies, 911: 11
Fire department: 106, 107, 108, 116
Health services: 63, 107, 108, 111, 122, 125, 130, 131, 160
Library: 106, 107, 108, 111, 116, 121, 149, 159
Police department: 106, 107, 111, 116, 121
Post office: 106, 107, 111, 113, 116, 121, 148, 149
Public transportation: 147, 150, 151, 153, 154, 155, 156, 161
Schools: 2, 6, 13, 159

EMPLOYMENT
Application forms: 143
Interviews: 139
Paychecks: 142
Professions: 6, 135, 137, 140, 141, 144, 145, 161
Skills: 138, 139, 158
Want ads: 140, 144
Tools and equipment: 6, 136, 144